Holland-America Line
AF344547

A Bridge To The Seven Seas

Dick Schaap & Dick Schaap

David McKay Company Inc.

New York

FOR REAL COMFORT
STATENDAM
HOLLAND-AMERICA LINE
Holland-America Line

Netherlands
American
NASM
STEAM NAVIGATION COMPANY
Royal
Mail service
between
ROTTERDAM
and
AMSTERDAM
New York

Holland-America Line
Rotterdam - Le Havre - Southampton - Cobh (Ireland) - New York and Canadian Ports

WIEN - NEW YORK
ÜBER ROTTERDAM
NASM
Doppelschraubendampfer
12500 Tonnen
HOLLAND-AMERIKA LINIE

DIE EVOLUTION IM TRANSPORTWESEN
1610 - 1910
HOLLAND-AMERIKA LINIE
ROTTERDAM - NEWYORK
über Boulogne sur Mer.

NETHERLANDS AMERICAN STEAM-
NAVIGATION COMPANY.
Royal & U.S.
Mail Steamers
ROTTERDAM
AMSTERDAM
NEW-YORK
VIA BOULOGNE SUR MER

NASM
Netherlands
American
Steam Navigation
Company

NEW YORK

REAL COMFORT
HOLLAND
AMERICA LINE
HOLLAND-AMERIKA
LINIE

NAAR AMERIKA CA...
CUBA EN MEXICO M...
HOLLAND
AMERIK...
LYN

Netherlands
American
Steam Navigation
Company
NASM
U.S. & Royal Mail
Steamers
ROTTERDAM
AMSTERDAM
New-York
via Boulogne sur Mer

Royal
Netherlands & U.S.
Mail Line
COMPANY'S
PASSENGER OFFICES
Picture from Holland

Holland-America Line

NETHERLANDS AMERICAN
STEAM NAVIGATION
Royal Netherlands and United...
Telegraphic
Address
AMERICANO
NETHERLAND
N.A.S.M.
Direct
Weekly service
between
ROTTERDAM
AMSTERDAM
and NEW-YORK

TRAVEL
Holland-America Line

Holland-America
Linie
N.A.S.M.
Rotterdam-
Newyork
via Boulogne-sur-M...

List of Members
CLARK'S
16TH ANNUAL
CRUISE
TO THE
MEDITERRANEAN
AND THE
ORIENT
INCLUDING SPAIN
Specially Chartered HOLLAND-AMERICA
S.S. ROTTERDAM
Feb. 2. 1914   24,170 TONS
A TOUR OF 64
OR 70 DAYS
SPENDING 16 DAYS IN
PALESTINE
AND
EGYPT
INCLUDING
SHORE EXCURSIONS, HOTELS,
DRIVES, FEES AND ALL
NECESSARY EXPENSES.

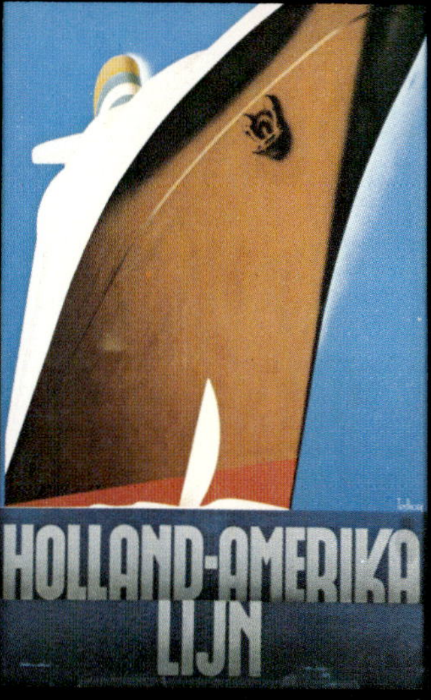

Chapter 1
People at Sea
page 4

Chapter 2
Bridge across
the Ocean
page 22

Chapter 3
Chicago Piano
page 44

Chapter 4
Years without Hope
page 70

Chapter 5
The Sea:
Source of Life
page 88

First published in The Netherlands 1973
by Meijer Pers bv, Amsterdam.
Copyright © 1973 by Meijer Pers bv,
Amsterdam, The Netherlands.
All rights reserved.
No part of this book may be reproduced
or utilized in any form or by
any means, electronic, or mechanical,
including photocopying, recording,
or by any information storage
and retrieval system,
without permission in writing
from the publisher.
Library of Congress Catalog
Card Number 73-80300.
Published in the United States in 1973,
by David McKay Company, Inc., New York.

s.s. Nieuw Amsterdam II/design Wim ten Broek/1950/poster detail

HOLLAND AMERICA'S S. S. NIEUW AMSTERDAM ANCHORS OFF ONE OF THE SOUTH AMERICAN ISLANDS UNDER THE CURIOUS EYES OF COLORFULLY DRESSED NATIVE FISHERMEN. NA-4

The s.s. *Nieuw Amsterdam* lay at anchor off the shore of the Isla de Margarita, a West Indian gem sparkling in the Caribbean. Tenders churned back and forth carrying passengers from their floating hotel to the tropical island. It was so peaceful, so quiet on the beach that the ringing of a bell aboard the ship could be heard clearly on the distant shore.

Thomas van Hall stood on the beach, scanning the exotic scene, his eyes half closed to fight off the fierce reflection of the sunlight from the crystal waters of the bay. Coconut palms swayed behind him. Half a century earlier, Thomas van Hall had sailed from Rotterdam to New York, a third-class passenger aboard an earlier *Nieuw Amsterdam*. Now, in the centennial year of the Holland America Line, Thomas van Hall was celebrating his own semi-centennial voyage; now he was a luxury passenger aboard a luxury ship, a ship he invariably called "The Grand Old Lady." He had spoken to me of his love for the sea, and I had asked him the basis of his love, and he was considering his answer.

I had my own thoughts, less lofty perhaps. "Beautiful woman, that South African," I mused. "Traveling around the world, she and her daughter. Kittenish. Intelligent. Well-read. What is her name? Elphia? It sounds like something lifted out of a fairy tale. Tonight, I want to dance with her on the promenade deck, in the Stuyvesant restaurant."

Thomas van Hall tapped me on the shoulder, interrupting my fantasy. "To me," he said, "sailing is like a life one has never lived — but a life whose existence one has always suspected." He was very serious. "It is," said Thomas van Hall, "a dream."

People at sea. Each has his own dreams, his own story. Ron Goodnight, for instance. Genial and broad-shouldered, a banker and a factory owner, above all a Texan. During the day, he slips into his diver's suit and plunges into the waters of the Caribbean, searching for lost treasure, as though it is something he finds every day. In the evenings, he swirls around the Ritz Carlton with his wife, Sue, impeccably dressed, impeccably manicured. They dominate the dance floor aboard the *Nieuw Amsterdam;* they compel attention. For Ron Goodnight, one of the virtues of being at sea is that he can escape the telephone, which rings incessantly at home. Still, even at sea, Ron Goodnight pauses daily at the ticker, studying the latest fluctuations of Wall Street. He can give up the phone, but he cannot give up everything.

The serious young blonde from Chicago. She dreads the moment when the ship will dock at Fort Lauderdale, the moment when her cruise will end. She savors each minute at sea. Every morning, she is one of the first passengers on deck. Her first sea voyage is an act of liberation; she is free of Chicago, free of the fears of the big city — where she never walks on the street alone at night, where the door to her apartment is secured with a chain and double lock.

The geologist from Houston, with his sun-tanned skin. He tells fascinating stories about expeditions for gold and silver in remote regions of South America. He goes to sea, he explains, because he feels so restless ashore.

The American citizen born in the Netherlands. John Last, a confirmed Calvinist, member of church committees, on the boards of several colleges, vice-president of a box-making plant in Wayne, New Jersey. He feels a bond among himself, the s.s. *Nieuw Amsterdam* and her owner, the Holland America Line. Last remembers, as if it were yesterday, his crossing to the New World aboard the first *Nieuw Amsterdam*, a fourmaster of 17,000 tons gross register. Last made the trip in September, 1918. "We had to sail through a mine field," he recalls. "The First World War was still going on. We held a prayer-meeting in the dining room, to pray for the safety of the ship and all aboard her. I was a boy of nine at the time. Nobody went to sleep that night. Everybody kept praying until the danger had passed. I can never forget that night."

The melancholy bartender, Lenny. He seems possessed by a sweet sadness; not long after he married, his young wife died in a car crash. Several years have passed, but she is still with him. In his cabin, deep within the ship, where you can hear the propellors of the 37,000-ton ship churning, he keeps a photograph of his dead wife on his desk. "That's what life can do to you," Lenny says. Caught up in the pace of the ship, he does not grieve openly; only a trace of sadness persists.

The incredibly busy little clothing manufacturer from New York. He will tell you, with little prompting, about his two million dollar annual turnover; he will also tell you that he finds everything on board lousy. He cannot find anything right with his cabin steward. In his luxury cabin, he wants to be able to press the button and have champagne and caviar appear at three in the morning.

The elderly American couple born in Luxembourg. He sits at a round table in the Champlain dining room, wearing a handsomely tailored white dinner jacket and pince-nez. His wife's gown is smart, yet dazzling. She underlines her former beauty with a single, stunning diamond. They are in their 60s, but they move with a restraint and a grace that indicates dignity and breeding.

The three American divorcees, still young, still dreaming. They dream of a shipboard adventure that will never happen, largely because, aboard the *Nieuw Amsterdam*, they don't lose sight of one another for even a moment.

The jovial priest with his bright blue Cary Grant eyes. With a wink, he lets it be known that he recognizes the dilemma of the three young divorcees. During the day, he relaxes on the Lido deck, his bathing suit laced with tiger stripes. At dinner, he gives away his profession with his neat, white dog collar.

Mary Ann from New Mexico, only seventeen and sensual. It is almost painful to watch the way she shows her passion for the handsome Norwegian singer who works with the band from Manilla. Her love is unrequited, but no matter. On her next voyage, she will fall madly in love once more, not with the

*1972

Roaming over exotic islands.
(Cuts from HAL-pamphlets.)
Shore leave on Martinique.
(Thomas van Hall.)

singer, but with the drummer, or perhaps the guitar player.

The chief steward from Rotterdam who has spent so many years at sea he has drifted away from his family, into less formal relationships. He reads and rereads the letters from his mistress, a voluptuous British singer. "God, what a wonderful woman she is!" he says, wistful and appreciative. He is well into his 50s; his children have grown up, and the youngest will be going to college this year. He has difficulty answering the letters of his wife. "Ought I to tell her?" he wonders.

The first mate, his uniform, his "djas toetoep," buttoned to the neck. One evening, he puts a typed booklet in my hands, a manuscript he has treasured for years. It was written in 1943, a description of "Activities in the Troop Kitchen of No. 5000," the wartime number of the s.s. *Nieuw Amsterdam*, converted for the duration into a troop carrier. No. 5000 carried eight thousand soldiers at a time on its military cruises, plying back and forth between New York and Europe, California and the Pacific, no time to pause for sightseeing. But even then, judging from the first mate's manuscript, the chef de cuisine tried to maintain the high standards of his kitchen. For a wartime Christmas, the chef served eight thousand soldiers a turkey dinner with all the trimmings, from vegetable soup to ice cream. "It took four days and three nights to roast all the turkeys," the first mate remembers.
Around him, people are eating caviar and sipping champagne.

Ships have a soul, the writer Nicholas Monsarrat suggests. And if you should trample on that soul, they can even sink of shame. When you roam through the elegant public rooms of the s.s. *Nieuw Amsterdam*, when you mingle with her crew, never obtrusive, yet never obsequious, you sense the soul of the ship. You cannot help but wonder at the stories you would hear if "The Grand Old Lady" could talk, and if she chose to reveal her secrets.

People at sea. They all have their own special memories, and often the memories, like the ship, form a bridge across the seas. Ron Goodnight, a Dallas Texan and proud of it, reveals after three glasses of Scotch-on-the-rocks that he did not spring straight from the Pecos or the panhandle. His ancestors were German colonists. The aristocratic couple in the Champlain dining room recall wine festivals long ago in Luxembourg. The geologist from Houston remembers his grandfather at family parties, singing Irish ballads in a rich, reverberating voice. A small, somewhat dark man with a beautiful Roman nose insists that no one in the world can match his mother's spaghetti sauce. The priest talks of his dream, to visit Ireland. The young woman from Chicago calls France her idea of paradise on earth.

On a cruise through the Caribbean, winding among the West Indian islands between Miami and Caracas, it is almost impossible to find an American passenger who does not feel a strong tie to the old world. And why not? Forty-four million people, Poles and Russians, Italians and Dutchmen, Irish and English, Scandinavians and Jews, the persecuted and the adventurous, men and women, people thirsting for freedom, all of them crossed the Atlantic to the United States after 1776. It was the largest exodus in the history of the world. Forty-four million people stepped onto the bridge across the seas. They, and their descendants, plowed the prairies, dug the canals, built the roads and the railways, worked in mines and factories and, together, built a free society. They demonstrated that a country could grow into a strong nation without one unifying religion or a common culture. I could read history, more vividly than from any book, in the faces and stories of those 800 passengers sailing aboard the s.s. *Nieuw Amsterdam*, herself an historical textbook.

Thomas van Hall is a walking history. He is 72 years old, and he still pursues life vigorously. He takes you to the market at Martinique and guides your taste to unfamiliar fruits; he bids you sample the exotic liqueurs at the House of Riise, the world's largest retail spirit shop, 100,000 bottles of strong drink from every country stored in a magnificent warehouse in Charlotte Amalie, St. Thomas.
He leads you to a Spanish cafe in Caracas and feeds you mangoes and papayas, cocoa beans and cinammon sticks, and, always, his stories of days gone by. Old Thomas is a man who lives by day. At night, when the others aboard the *Nieuw Amsterdam* are dancing and sipping cocktails and listening till early in the morning to the wistful sounds of a Rumanian pianist, Thomas sleeps. But he is up at dawn, still anxious to

NIEUW AMSTERDAM II HOLLAND AME

crowd every experience into his 73rd year.

Shipping. A bridge to the seven seas. A bridge, especially, across the Atlantic. On a clear evening, under a starlit sky, if you let your imagination go, you can listen to the humming of the turbines, the churning of the propellors and you can hear them singing.

We took all those people to America — Einstein and Carnegie, Sikorsky and Fermi, Astor and Alexander Graham Bell, Toscanini, Sarnoff, Steinmetz, Mergenthaler, Sabin, DuPont, an endless list, all passing through Ellis Island.

Nowadays, Ellis Island is a forlorn, rundown place, diagonally opposite the lower tip of Manhattan Island. But from 1892 to 1943, Ellis Island was the most important gateway to America. It bears the name of a wealthy merchant from Manhattan who owned the island at the start of the eighteenth century. Anny Moore, from Cork, Ireland, was the first immigrant to be cleared through Ellis Island. To commemorate the occasion, she received a ten dollar bill from the authorities. In the days of the "Great Immigration," shortly after the start of the twentieth century, more than 5,000 immigrants a day reached Ellis Island.

Thomas van Hall still remembers the island clearly. He landed there in 1923. "I took

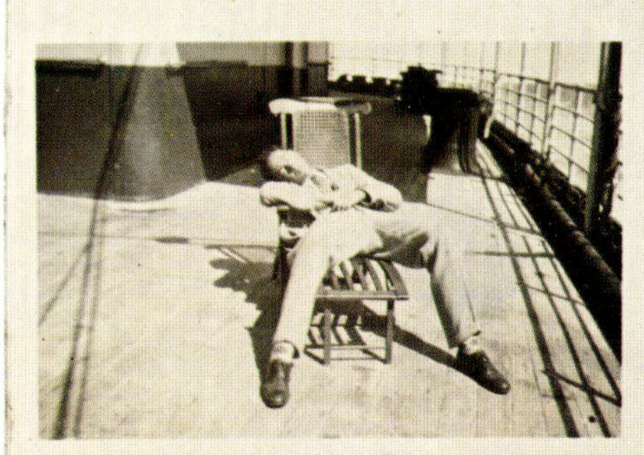

An emigrant's family album. Single journey Rochester. Thomas van Hall in his first tin lizzie. Acting as master of ceremonies during a mock wedding on board.

pot luck,'' he says. ''I wasn't doing too badly in Holland. I had finished my studies at the School of Agriculture in Wageningen, and I was earning 30 guilders a week in Amsterdam. But I wanted to get away. The landscape gardener and architect, Kraayenbrink, the chief gardener for Queen Wilhelmina, lent me the money for the crossing. It was quite a trip. We were seated twelve to a table in third class. At the head of the table sat an enormous glutton. The chief steward put the pan of stew in front of him every day. And every day he ate all of it himself. Finally, I asked the steward, 'Can't you put that pan in front of me for a change? Then we can all have at least a little.'

''The people in steerage had an even more difficult time. They crossed the ocean with a $30 ticket. Packed closely together, they sat on their suitcases and baskets tweendecks. Early each morning, they were sent to the open deck so that the crew could clean out the steerage quarters thoroughly.

My wife came to America with her parents in 1910. She was only four years old then. I still have to laugh when she tells me what happened on Ellis Island. In the crowd there, she was mistakenly assigned to a group of Polish immigrants. Her mother screamed at my wife's father, 'Jaap, Sientje is walking there among the immigrants!' The father screamed back, with some irritation, 'Woman, who do you think you are? I suppose you are not an immigrant?'''

Ellis Island. Just past the Statue of Liberty. The steerages, weighed down by memories of the countries they had left, often cried when they saw the Statue, the symbol of their new land. The tenders *Wm. Fletcher* and *John E. Moore* carried hundreds of thousands of immigrants to and from the island; today they lie in front of the main building, idle and rusty, of no use since the building shut down in 1954. The last passenger aboard the tenders was a Norwegian sailor who had deserted ship. He was sent back to his own country in November, 1954. His name was Arne Petersson, and The New York Times wrote of him in an article entitled ''Last Man Off Ellis Island.''

EMPIRE DES MERS & OCEANS
ARCHIDIOCESE DE LA LIGNE

CERTIFICAT DE BAPTEME DE LA LIGNE

Nous, PETRUS POMPILIUS,
PROTONOTAIRE DE SA MAJESTE
NEPTUNE
EMPEREUR ET ROI DES OCEANS

certifions que le Néophyte :

Stapel . C

franchissant l'EQUATEUR en ce 10ème jour d'Oc-
tobre de l'An de grâce 1940, à bord du Noble Vais-
seau des FORCES LIBRES „WESTERNLAND" a été
baptisé selon nos Rites en présence de Notre Cour,
avec l'Onction salée habituelle et la Plus Grande
Pompe du Bord.

LE PERE LA LIGNE

HOLLAND-AMERICA LINE
RED STAR LINE SERVICE

Crossing the equator.

*1940

*1930

SWIMMINGPOOL BEING
...[CLE.. SWIMMERS ARE
...RNESTLY ADVISED TO
...RAIN FROM DIVING.

Ellis Island. Small wooden nameplates, inscriptions, names scratched into wood — they remain to remind us of the millions who once arrived on the island for examination and inspection. They had to form lines of 30 in front of the immigration officers in the main building. The inspection was both strict and efficient. The slightest sign of ill health was enough for the doctors of the United States Public Health Service to chalk a mark on the steerage and separate him or her from the healthy. People with ringworm, leprosy, trachoma or venereal disease were immediately returned to their native countries; they never got to see more of America than the silhouette of Manhattan. Anarchists, polygamists and lawbreakers were also screened out.

Most of the immigrants were relatively unschooled and unskilled. East European intellectuals and white-collar workers had a very difficult time emigrating; their own countries refused to let them go. The Holland America Line representative in Warsaw found a way around the problem. A rough stone was set in the ground in front of his office. Then, the HAL representative inspected the hands of all aspiring emigrants. If he found the smooth hands of a clerical worker, he sent the man outside to rub his palms — and especially his fingernails — across the rough stone for perhaps ten minutes. The man then stood a better chance of receiving the coveted visa for the United States.

To many immigrants, the arrival at the main building preceded a stay of many months on Ellis Island. They had to wait until relatives found work for them — or could put up enough money to guarantee their upkeep for a while. To those stranded on Ellis Island, it was a miserable place. And the shipping companies who had brought over the stranded immigrants suffered, too. They could forget about any profit on the small steerage fare; they were responsible for the feeding of the immigrants who could not leave the island.

"I wasn't an expensive lodger for the Holland America Line," says Thomas van Hall with a grin, as he sits in his comfortable cabin

Ellis Island, just past the
Statue of Liberty,
is now a desolate and
forlorn spot.

aboard the *Nieuw Amsterdam*. "I went straight from New York to Rochester. And I have lived there ever since. There I got married, and there my children were born.
"I still remember the strange names people on Ellis Island had for their destinations in the United States. Somebody said he was going to Linkinbra; he meant Lincoln, Nebraska. Detroit, Michigan, became Detrayamis, and Des Moines, Iowa, was Dees Moyness, Yova. What did we know about America? Only one thing: the country is rich enough and big enough to give us all work — and it guarantees our freedom."

⛵   Thomas van Hall had one friend in Rochester, New York, but at the beginning, Thomas found life difficult. He worked for a while on a big farm, barely earning his room and board, and finally, in desperation, he decided to volunteer for the U.S. Army. With a small suitcase in his hand, he walked one morning through a quiet street in Rochester. As he passed a factory, a man called out to him, "Where are you going so early in the morning?" "To the Army recruiting office," said Thomas. Thomas told the man that he had to eat somehow, and the man took Thomas to his boss at the factory. "Haven't you got any work for him?" the man said. "The poor man's so desperate he's ready to join the Army." Thomas van Hall got a job at the factory. "I've been grateful to that man ever since," Thomas says. "I've grown to love Rochester and America. In Rochester, I have become head of the water works — all because I had considerable knowledge of gardening and the city engineer felt I was capable of going to college and learning something about drinking water."

⛵   People at sea. The people of America. "A great deal has changed in a century," says John Last, as we stand by the docks in Caracas, watching containers being loaded aboard a modern freighter. Last is a real ship-lover, and he prides himself upon his knowledge of shipping and ships, old and modern. "When I crossed the Atlantic in 1918," he says, "the

Nieuw Amsterdam still had a full complement of sails on board. They were never used, but they were there. Did you know that it wasn't until 1873 that a regular steamship connection between the Netherlands and America came into being? That was the beginning of the Holland America Line. Before then, the Dutch connection with North America was maintained only by sailing ships. The voyage from Rotterdam to America took six to twelve weeks. There was no question of traveling in comfort. My father, a carpenter, could spin some yarns about the voyages. He was a restless man and he simply signed on as ship's carpenter whenever he got it into his head to settle in some distant land. His bags were always packed. On those sailing ships, the ones he went on, the passengers' quarters were always cramped. There was no ventilation. The food was bad and insufficient. There were no decent sanitary arrangements. Infectious diseases were common aboard ship. Once, when my father sailed to Cuba, the ship was jammed with corpses. My father was kept very busy, making slides to commit the covered-up corpses 'one, two, three — in God's name —' to the deep."

⛵   Even though there was no steamship service to North America till the 1870s, there was a regular steamship service between the Netherlands and Paramaribo as early as 1827. It was a state packet-boat service, a project endorsed by King William I. The service was maintained by H. M. Steam Packet *Curaçao*, the first ship to cross the Atlantic in both directions under steam. It was truly a remarkable achievement. As late as 1835, a British expert called the possibility of a direct steamship connection between Liverpool and New York — a distance of 3,100 nautical miles — only a figment of the imagination. Yet the *Curaçao* was already making the 3,900-mile trip from the Netherlands to Paramaribo.
Nowadays, I know, you can fly by 747 from New York to Amsterdam in seven hours. The managing director of KLM Royal Dutch Airlines — Plesman — was right when he said, shortly after World War II, that ships would play no part

in passenger traffic across the Atlantic within ten years. He was slightly off on his timing, but he was right on his theory.

⛵   Still, I doubt that the big liners — ships such as the *Nieuw Amsterdam*, *Statendam*, *Rotterdam*, *Volendam* and *Veendam*, and the big British, Italian, Norwegian and American vessels — will ever disappear from the sea. The airplane and the ship complement each other beautifully. You can fly to Singapore, and the Holland America Line will have a ship waiting there to take you on a cruise through the Indonesian Archipelago. What could be more ideal for someone in this hectic world than a leisurely holiday aboard a cruise ship? Flying is for moving from one place to another; sailing is traveling, in the best sense of the word. Once a person has discovered the sea he is never quite able to turn his back on it completely.

⛵   John Last, obviously, has found success in America; he credits much of his success to the fact that he made the crossing aboard the old *Nieuw Amsterdam* when he was only a child. "I can still see myself with my mother arriving in New York on that big ship," he says. "We berthed at Pier 46, near the Chelsea docks. My father was already in America. He had emigrated from Cuba to America, and he had found work in Paterson, New Jersey.

⛵   "I grew up in New Jersey, and it was a good childhood. The Reverend Hames, a Reform minister who considered it his duty to visit and help Dutch people, immediately made us welcome in Paterson. I was sent to a Christian school founded by Dutch people; there were 500 children in the school and we studied Dutch one hour a week. We got a good education, and some of those children who studied with me are still among my closest friends.

⛵   "We got through the Depression well. My father took a job as janitor for a block of apartment houses during those dreadful years. At least we had a roof over our heads, and we had free washing facilities. My mother always felt that the grass in Holland was greener than the grass anywhere else in the world.

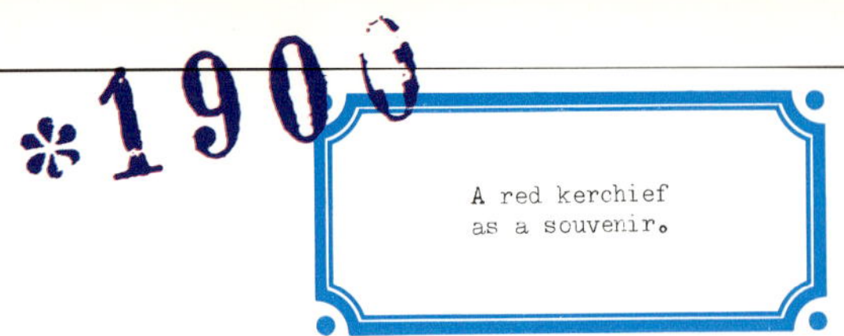
*1900
A red kerchief
as a souvenir.

VIENNA
BERLIN
LEIPSIC

CHICAGO
BOSTON
ST.LOUIS

HOLLAND AMERICA LINE

NEW YORK

NEW YORK

New Twinscrew Steamers
12500 TONS

JE MAINTIENDRAI

BRÜNN
INNSBRUCK
TRIEST

PARIS
BOULOGNE SUR MER
GENEVA

ROTTERDAM AMSTERDAM

She always dreamed of going back. Yet, finally, when she did go back, she found that she no longer felt at home there. She is still alive, at 92, and she is happy with her children and her grandchildren.

"My father, as I've told you, was a real traveler, a man who went to sea on the slightest excuse. Once he was visiting someone's home in the Netherlands and he saw on the mantelpiece a photograph of a beautiful girl. He fell in love with the photograph. 'Who is that?' he asked. 'That is Marie Vegersteen,' he was told, 'but you'll never meet her. She lives now in the Argentine.' A week later, my father signed aboard a boat bound for South America. And he went to the Argentine and met Marie Vegersteen and married her. She is my mother. I was born in the Argentine. Isn't that a romantic story?"

People at sea. People from everywhere. People with stories. At the end of the journey aboard the *Nieuw Amsterdam,* the hot tempered clothing manufacturer walks up to the captain from Zeeland and the hotel manager from Haarlem and says, "I still think everything's lousy, but I have to admit it keeps looking better. The Farewell Dinner was fantastic, and the Crew Show was exciting. It didn't bore me for a minute. It never entered my mind that those marvelous dancers from Bali were actually Indonesian cabin stewards dressed as women. It was terrific."

The married couple from Luxembourg are close to tears at the Farewell Dinner when a choir of Dutch and Indonesian stewards starts to sing, "When the time comes to say goodbye," and flaming ice-cakes are carried into the dining room. The couple intend to book again the following year. They have heard the rumor that the s.s. *Nieuw Amsterdam* may soon be retired from service and they hope it is untrue. "We should hate it if this ship had to be broken up," says the husband. "There should be a special law to forbid it."

The priest has become a ship-lover for life. He has made friends with the cruise's rabbi, a man with reddish hair, an attractive wife and four noisy children. Thomas van Hall offers a story appropriate to the friendship between the priest and the rabbi. "You know," says Thomas, "I sing operettas in my spare time. I have a very good voice. On my next-to-last trip aboard this ship, the rabbi came up to me and asked if I would serve as his cantor during the religious services. He hadn't been able to find a Jewish passenger with a good voice. I said, 'But i don't know anything about the services.' The rabbi said, 'I'll teach you in a jiffy.' And he did. I'm a Christian, but I found the experience quite interesting. My wife was a little bit upset by it. She's a bit of a church-goer, you know." Thomas pulls out a small pile of yellowed snapshots, showing him as master of ceremonies aboard the *Ryndam.* "That was in 1926," he says, "on our honeymoon."

The three young divorcees offer emotional goodbyes to all the people they met during the cruise. For them, the trip was too short. They would have liked to have danced much longer with the ship's officers.

Ron Goodnight walks down the gang-way in Fort Lauderdale, waving his farewells to everyone. He has invited half the ship's passengers and half the crew to visit him in Texas.

The captain of the *Nieuw Amsterdam* shakes hands with as many people as possible. "Did you enjoy yourself?" he asks. Quickly, he is called aside by the shore agent who is ready with the passenger list for the next cruise. "This is what this business is like," says the captain. "You have to be the captain and a good host at the same time." He is an admirer of Michiel Adriaansz de Ruyter, the greatest admiral in Dutch maritime history; in his cabin, he keeps an engraving of de Ruyter. "Bestevaer de Ruyter never let anything upset him," the captain says. "He was a courteous man. He was a good person."

The young blonde from Chicago stands on the dock, hesitating. "Thanks for the talks we had," she says. "Perhaps there's still some hope for humanity. Perhaps I have been looking at everything too gloomily." She smiles easily now.

The geologist from Houston is grumbling at the customs officer who is levying a sizable tax on the excess bottles of whiskey brought in from the island of St. Thomas. "Why bother with the tax?" says the geologist. "They're much more understanding in South America." "Then go live in South America," suggests the customs officer.

The chief steward from Rotterdam is still torn between his family and his lady friend from England. "Next month I'm due for leave," he says. "What should I do? Rotterdam or London? Should I tell my wife or shouldn't I?"

Lenny the bartender dismisses the problem. "There are people who always manage to get themselves into a fix," he says. "They can't live without it." Lenny smiles his sad smile. "Give my love to everybody in New York and Rotterdam," he says, "and everywhere else on shore. You're sure to come across someone who knows me. Drink my health with a glass of beer. I'd rather stay on board."

Humming, Lenny sets to work, polishing his bar, arranging his glasses, getting everything ready for the next shipload of passengers. He hopes to find some friends among them. In fact, he is positive that he will.

NASM
Wekelijksche Vaart met de Stoomsche
Nederlandsch-Amerikaansch
Stoomvaart Maatschap
Rotterdam.
Billetten worden naar alle plaatsen der Vereenigde Staten afgegeven.

s.s. W. A. Scholten / 1880 / poster detail

BRIDGE ACROSS THE OCEAN

The Europe of 1900 in a
bilingual guide for emigrants.
Poland has been partitioned
by Russia, Germany (Posen),
Austria (Galicia).

HOLLAND-AMERIKA LINIE
ROTTERDAM — NEW-YORK.
Führer für Dampfschiff-Reisende III. Classe
aus Ungarn und Galizien nach Nord-Amerika
mittelst der Holland-Amerika Linie
(Niederländisch-amerikanische Dampfschiffahrts-Gesellschaft.)
Kanzleien der Gesellschaft für Reisende III. Classe in Wien:
IV., Weyringergasse 7a und II., Kaiser Josefstrasse 36.
Wien 1900.
Verlag der Gesellschaft.

*1900

Uebersichtskarte der Reise von Ungarn und Galizien über Wien nach Rotte
Magyarországból és Galicziából Bécsen keresztül Rotterdamba való utazásnak átnéz

Uebersichtskarte der Reise von Wien über Rotterdam nach New-York. (Siebenmal so klein
Bécsből Rotterdamon keresztül New-Yorkba való utazásnak átnézeti kártyája. (Hétszer kisebb

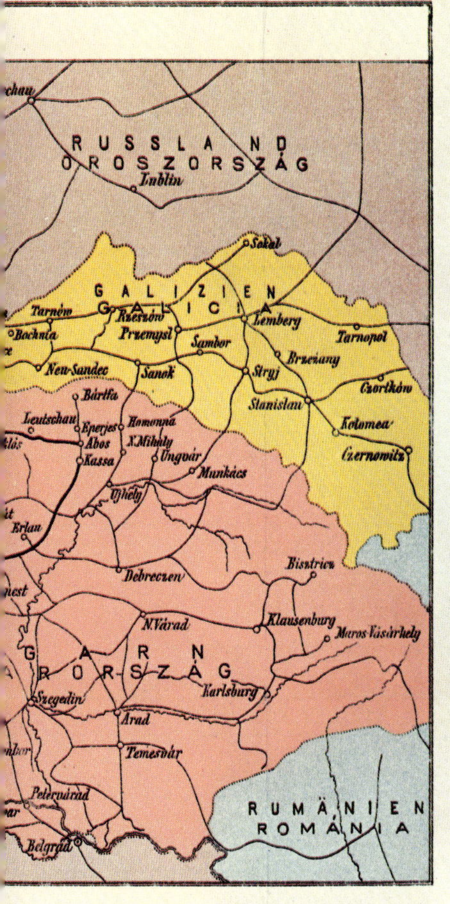

Watch a child folding a piece of paper into a little ship. It is so human, so natural. For thousands of years, man has built himself ships. It is his oldest means of transportation — the first real successor to his own two feet. Before he managed to tame horses and donkeys and camels, before he invented the wheel and with it the cart, before he even dreamed of flying, man built his sailing vessels: Rafts of reed and twigs and branches. Later, he began to scoop out tree trunks; the ship was born.

With their ships, Greeks and Romans maneuvered their legions and traded their wares around the Mediterranean. Seamanship was so much a part of the ancient world that the legendary Ulysses was startled when the gods ordered him to go plant an oar in the ground of a country whose people did not know ships. With their ships, the Vikings, driven by poverty, sailed to the Low Countries.

With their ships, discoverers explored the world: Columbus, admiral of the ocean; Amerigo Vespucci, the man who may have beaten Columbus to the New World; Leif Ericson, Vasco de Gama, Hendrik de Zeevaarder, Magellen, Ponce de Leon. So many others. With their ships, they built a bridge across the seven seas and linked the continents.

Until the nineteenth century, sails dominated the seas. Countless sea shanties recall the aimless drifting of becalmed ships; countless others remember the sails battered in gales off the treacherous Cape Horn. Every lover of ships knows the stories about the old Cape Horn mariners, about their struggles against the terrors of Tierra del Fuego, the Strait of Magellen and the tumultous seas of the Cape.

On June 27, 1898, Captain Joshua Slocum ended his dramatic one-man voyage around the world aboard the cutter *Spray*. On February 19, 1896, more than two years earlier, he had set sail for Cape Horn from Sandy Point (Punta Arena), in those days a Chilean fueling station. Two months later, he made the following entry in his diary: "'Hurray for the *Spray!*' I shouted to the seals, sea gulls and penguins. For now she had braved all the dangers of Cape Horn, and no other human beings were near."

A few lines later, he wrote: "In the evening, a wave — bigger than any that had threatened me that day — a wave of the kind seafaring folk call 'fair-weather seas' broke fore and aft over the cutter. I, too, got my share of it. To me, it appeared to be a final expression of regret."

Life on the last big sailing vessels was rather easygoing and informal. Voyages often lasted months, and the passengers amused themselves with games, embroidery and theatrical entertainment, pretty much as they do today on shorter voyages. The Crew Show then was a daily event, unrehearsed and unstaged. The sailors sang shanties to keep up their spirits and coordinate their efforts while pulling ropes and hauling sheets.

The sailor with the best voice would sing one or two lines solo. Then the rest of the crew would join in the chorus, at the same time flinging themselves into their work.

To help pass the long voyages, good food and good drink was essential. The bill of fare on the old sailing ships was plain by modern standards, but substantial. Fruit was missing from the menu; tinned fruit did not yet exist, and the fresh variety would spoil too quickly. But flour was carried for the baking of bread, and there were plenty of potatoes, carrots and onions. Dutch sailing ships carrying passengers often carried a cow as well so that there could be at least an occasional ration of milk. Some of the ships brought along their own livestock — chickens, pigs and cheap sheep from Australia; very few of the livestock, for the obvious reason, survived the ocean crossing.

The main meals for the cabin passengers included, as a rule:
Green or yellow peas with salted meat.
Salted fish.
Pickled cabbage with bacon and potatoes.
Pea soup with pickled beef.
Salted haricot beans and stringbeans with sausage.
White beans with ham.

*1886

From time to time, chicken, pork and salted salmon also were served. For dessert, the passengers depended on rice with currants, groats with prunes, dried apples and dried pears – all a far cry from today's flaming baked Alaska.

Life aboard the last of the big sailing vessels changed dramatically in the mid-nineteenth century as the emigration to America swelled. Millions of impoverished people from all parts of Western Europe sought to cross the Atlantic at the lowest possible cost. The lowest possible cost meant steerage. Between 1840 and 1860, nearly four million Europeans emigrated to America, and the vast majority traveled steerage.

Steerage. The word was enough to cause the emigrants shivers of fear. Some didn't know what they were getting into, but many had heard the tales of horror. The rate of mortality among the emigrants jammed into steerage quarters often exceeded ten per cent. The steerage quarters usually were only five feet high and only in rare cases was there any ventilation. Steerage passengers generally prepared their own food in their own cramped and stale quarters. Seasickness, hunger, typhus, dysentery, even outbreaks of madness turned the voyage to the New World into a nightmare.

In Shakespeare's "Tempest," Gonzalo, the aged counsellor, cries, "Now would I give a

Emigrants from
Hungary and Yugoslavia.

thousand furlongs of sea for an acre of barren ground — long heath, brown furze, anything." Gonzalo must have been traveling steerage; the word became a term of opprobrium for the millions of emigrants who crossed the ocean tweendecks, paying thirty or thirty-five dollars for the dubious privilege. One survivor of steerage, William Smith, recorded his experiences on board the sailing vessel *India*, crossing from Liverpool to New York in the winter of 1847–48. The voyage lasted eight weeks, and the bitter story is called, "An Emigrant's Narrative: Or a Voice From the Steerage."

On Friday, November 26, Smith reports, the *India* sets sail with 300 steerage passengers, most of them Irish and poor. The passengers have few provisions; they have been waiting in Liverpool a fortnight for the departure of their ship. Immediately, the *India* sails into a heavy gale, and as the ship rolls and trembles, the barrels and cases of the passengers — apparently not lashed down securely — break loose. Within minutes, nothing remains of the barrels and cases but a heap of splintered wood, surrounded by drenched and ruined coffee, tea, sugar, potatoes, spiced meat, trousers, shirts and vests. "The cries of the women and children was heart-rending," William Smith recounts, "some praying, others weeping bitterly, as they saw their provisions and clothes — the only property they possessed — destroyed."

Halfway across the Atlantic, typhus breaks out aboard the *India*. A few passengers lose their sanity, jump overboard and drown. The master of the ship dies. The supply of drinking water gives out. William Smith finds himself so weak he can barely crawl onto the deck for occasional whiffs of sea air. Finally, two months after leaving Liverpool, the survivors spot land. They weap, they dance, they shout, they fall on their knees, thanking God that they have survived. "Thus was this disastrous journey at an end," writes William Smith. "My whole lifetime did not seem so long as the last two months appeared to me."

Kitchen equipment of a passenger ship. Menus with critical comments. Pantry third-class Rotterdam IV.
HOLLAND-AMERIKA LINE
SPEISEKARTE
TOURISTS
S.S. "ROTTERDAM" AUGUST 16, 1931
Very good
Table d'hôte
French
HOLLAND-AMERICA LINE
MENU
TOURISTS
S.S. "ROTTERDAM" AUGUST 18,
DINNER
Cream à l'Indienne   Bad
Boiled Flounder   Egg sauce
Steamed Potatoes
Roast Quarter of Pork with Gravy
Young Carrots   Château Potatoes
Ice-Cream
Mazurka Cake
Fruit   Coffee
HOLLAND-AMERICA LINE
MENU
TOURISTS
S.S. "ROTTERDAM" AUGUST 19, 1931
DINNER
Celery   Olives   Sardines
Cream à la Reine   BAD
Round of Beef with Gravy
Asparagus Hollandaise sauce   Roast Potatoes
Roast Chicken   Compote
Lettuce Salad French dressing
Ice Cream
Mocka Cake
Fruit   Coffee
AMERICA LINE
MENU
TOURISTS
"ROTTERDAM" AUGUST 18, 1931
LUNCHEON
St. Germain
Schnitzel
Sauté Potatoes
Meat with Pickles
Tomato Salad
Cheese   Jams
Pudding
Fruit
Bread and Butter
Coffee   Tea
bread a little stale today.
1931
1900

Then, suddenly, in the second half of the nineteenth century, the whole picture of emigration changed. Steam power arrived, freeing man of his dependence upon the vagaries of the wind, and the time and the danger of the Atlantic crossing were both reduced. The first steamships had been launched a little earlier, the *Savannah* in 1818, the *Defiance* in 1816, the *Curaçao* in 1827, but it wasn't until halfway through the century that the shipping industry stood on the brink of its modern system, a system in which the exact hour of arrival in New York — from Rotterdam or Amsterdam or Le Havre — can be anticipated.

"Steam power, that mighty lever of this day and age in almost any field, also makes it easier for the emigrant to carry out his plans to move," stated a handbook for emigrants published shortly after the 1873 founding of the Netherlands-American Steamship Company (which evolved into the Holland America Line). "Once on board," the handbook continued, "the emigrant finds his place waiting for him, where he will be billeted during the *short crossing*; that place has been provided for him in accordance with standards laid down by the government. It shall be separated from the engine room by a bulkhead, and it shall be a minimum distance from the engine room; within that place, no freight or goods shall be stowed.

"The berths are constructed in such a way that each person has sufficient length and width not to be thrown from his bed (and violently wake his neighbor) when the ship rolls heavily. The height of the berths, too, has been laid down, and it is forbidden to have more than two berths on top of each other.

"The simpler the bed is, the better; it need be used only for about a *fortnight*. Where there are so many people crowded together, cleanliness should prevail, and everybody should take care to air his mattress, pillow and blanket on deck as often as possible. Moreover, each emigrant should take care to keep his place clean; the necessary cleaning materials will be available on board."

The first HAL office at
Prins Hendrikkade 7, Rotterdam.
(Illustration from a guide for
emigrants.)
Holland America Line at
39 Lower Broadway, New York.

With the arrival of the steamships, the menu at sea changed, too. A shorter journey meant more fresh provisions, which meant, in turn, a more varied and wholesome cuisine. By 1896, the seagoing culinary arts had reached the point where a first-class cabin passenger traveling on the Holland America Line could expect the following dishes:

Breakfast:

Oatmeal, hominy, barley, hominy cakes, boiled, fried and poached eggs; ham and eggs, bacon and eggs, ham omelettes, cheese omelettes, jam omelettes, beefsteak, veal cutlets, mutton chops, chopped steak; boiled, fried, baked and mashed potatoes; Saratoga chips, fresh and pickled herring, sardines, smoked beef, ham and oxtongue, cold meats, assorted cheeses, crackers, biscuits, tea, coffee, cocoa, fruit.

Luncheon:

Brown bean soup, beefsteak, French fried potatoes, lobster salad, mayonnaise, apple dumplings, assorted cheeses, cold dishes, coffee, tea.

Dinner:

Oysters on the half shell, oxtail soup, spinach, macaroni au gratin, boiled oxtongue, hollandaise sauce, breasts of mutton, capers, duck, cabinet pudding, rum sauce, fruit desserts.

LOWER BROADWAY, 1899; Holland-America Line office was then at No. 39. Present location, at No. 29, was originally Columbia Building, first on left.

±1900

In all fairness, it should be noted that there were very few first-class cabin passengers aboard the early steamships. The staples of the shipping trade, the supports of the bridge across the Atlantic, were the freight traffic and the emigrant traffic. The emigrants did not enjoy the lush cuisine provided first-class passengers, but they were still vastly better off than their predecessors in the sailing ships. The emigrants no longer had to provide and prepare their own food on the steamships. On the first Holland America Line steamships, the emigrants received solid and even slightly varied nourishment. According to the rules and regulations of purser H. H. van den Toorn, the daily midday meal for emigrants included:

Monday: Sauerkraut, smoked bacon, potatoes, plum duff.
Tuesday: Pea soup, salted bacon, potatoes.
Wednesday: Brown bean soup, salted meat, potatoes, groats and raisins.
Thursday: Vegetable soup, beef with potatoes, rice with currants.
Friday: Pea soup, salted bacon, potatoes.
Saturday: White bean soup, salted meat, potatoes, groats with prunes.
Sunday: Vegetable soup, beef with potatoes, rice with currants.

Dining room of emigrants'
hotel.
Insets:
Dormitory for men.
Fumigator.

Bier per Glas | Pivo za pohar
Beer per glass | Pivo po staklo
Birra per bicchiere | Pivo za szklanke
Sör poharanként | בער פער גלאס
5 CENTEN - 2 DOLLAR CENTS
= 10 PFENNIG - 10 HELLER =
5 KOPEKEN.
Bier per Glas | Pivo za pohar
Beer per glass | Pivo po staklo
Birra per bicchiere | Pivo za szklanke
Sör poharanként
5 CENTEN 2 DOLLAR
10 PFENNIG 10
5 KOPEK

One passenger who crossed the Atlantic with the Holland America Line in the closing decades of the nineteenth century was a man named J. van 't Lindenhout. He offered a glowing, written endorsement for the journey: "I traveled aboard the steamship *Scholten* and wish to express my deep satisfaction with the way in which the captain and his officers treated us. Everything I saw aboard ship met with my satisfaction. The food, even for the tweendecks passengers, was excellent; it surprised me that such good food could be provided for such a low fare. Everything was so efficient that I heartily recommend the steamships of the Netherlands-American Steamship Company. It is very helpful to emigrants from our country to sail to America aboard a ship guided by Dutch officers, Dutch officers familiar with American customs; this enables the emigrants to learn gradually what they will encounter in America."

That endorsement was no isolated example. In the handbook for emigrants, put out by the Holland America Line, the following note appeared: "The undersigned, all passengers aboard the steamship *Rotterdam* of the Netherlands-American Steamship Company, sailing from Rotterdam to New York, herewith express their satisfaction with the kind treatment, the order and cleanliness to be found tweendecks and the sufficient quantities and good quality of the food supplied.

"On board steamship *Rotterdam,* June 25, 1887.

"The tweendecks passengers,

C. de Vries and wife

D. Bregman and wife

J. Bregman

A. Bakker

J. W. Bintentijd

P. van der Weel

P. Wette

C. Kaayman

C. Koer Wzoon

A. Bregman

A. Huibregtse

C. v. Driel

Geertruida Engelsman

Lena Wielaard Engelsman."

During the peak years of the early twentieth century emigration — concentrated in the years 1903 to 1907 and 1910 to 1915 — the steamship companies were kept busy and profitable carrying steerage passengers to America. In the first two decades of the present century, approximately twelve and a half million Europeans made the pilgrimage; the list included more than three million Italians, more than three million from the Balkan countries, two and a half million from Russia and the Baltic nations, almost a million from Britain and almost another million from Scandinavia, half a million Irish, half a million Germans and more than a million from the other European nations. Between 85 and 90 per cent of the emigrants made the journey to the New World tweendecks — as steerage or third-class passengers. Sometimes the big steamships carried as many as two or three thousand passengers, people who had sold their meager possessions in Europe and were hoping to begin a new life in a new world, armed only with a steerage ticket and their own talents and ambitions.

Wars, hunger, poverty and political and religious persecution and pogroms drove these millions from Europe to America. People from the Balkans and Turkey sailed to the United States from Constantinople, from Piraeus in Greece and from Trieste and Fiume on the Adriatic Sea. Italians sailed from Palermo or Taormina on Sicily or from Naples or Genoa on the mainland. A second stream of emigrants — from Eastern Europe — followed a northern route, through Russia to the Baltic or through Germany to the North Sea ports of Hamburg, Bremen, Rotterdam and Antwerp. Special emigrant trains served the ports. The period of waiting before the ship sailed, usually no more than a couple of days, was spent in hotels and inns owned and operated by the shipping lines. The Hamburg-America Line, for instance, operated the famous ''Auswander Hallen,'' buildings which could hold four thousand emigrants. Older people in Rotterdam can still recall vividly the arrival of emigrants from Eastern Europe. The men often had dark beards and wore large, black hats; the women wore wide skirts and shawls covered their heads. Officials of the Holland America Line, recognizable by their badge in the shape of the green white green houseflag, sheltered emigrants in a hotel built in 1893 on the Wilhelmina Quay in Rotterdam. That hotel could accommodate four hundred emigrants. There was a chapel within the hotel, and for Jewish emigrants, kosher meals were specially prepared.

The Dutch, infact, were late starters among the steamship companies carrying emigrant traffic. Before 1870, most of the traffic was handled by German shipping lines. The Dutch had been pioneers with the governmental steampacket service to Paramaribo, but they lagged behind when it came to building the steamship bridge from Rotterdam to New York.

Other countries bolted ahead of the Dutch. As early as 1840, the British & North American Royal Mail Steam Packet Company

New York (cover HAL-pamphlet).
Old picture cards:
New York,
pier foot of 5th Street.
Rotterdam,
Wilhelminakade with HAL office
and emigrants' hotel.

was in operation, founded by Samuel Cunard; later, the company became the Cunard Line, present-day owners of the *Queen Elizabeth II*. The Hamburg-American Line was born with sailing ships in 1847, converted to steam three years later and offered regular service between Hamburg and New York. In 1858, the Germans added the Norddeutscher Lloyd line of Bremen.

At the beginning, all the shipping companies faced financial problems, but as the number of emigrants rapidly increased, the lines started to flourish. In 1864, the Norddeutscher Lloyd, for instance, declared a ten per cent dividend; two years later, the dividend had climbed to twenty per cent.

The people in the Netherlands realized there was money and prestige to be made in transatlantic shipping, but the country suffered from an atmosphere of depression. The people who had once made the Republic of the United Netherlands the strongest trading and shipping nation in the world, who had founded the city of New Amsterdam on Manhattan Island, had become thoroughly disheartened. Trade with America was declining. Poverty and unemployment were widespread. The ports were in a scandalous state of decay. The Continental System, initiated under the reign of Napoleon, had taken its toll on Dutch shipping. Little was done to develop steam navigation because the Nederlandsche Handel-Maatschappij (Netherlands Trading Company), recovering from the impact of French rule, allowed the interests of sail to prevail. It is true that in Amsterdam there existed the Koninklijke Nederlandsche Stoomboot Maatschappij (Royal Netherlands Steamship Company), which was founded in 1856 and maintained service to European ports with sizable ships. KNSM considered itself the appropriate company to provide shipping service to New York, but KNSM hesitated, fearful that it would prove impossible to raise the needed capital in the Netherlands.

In 1823, a former Dutch naval officer named Gerhard Moritz Röntgen initiated the establishment of the Nederlandsche Stoomboot Maatschappij (the Netherlands Steamship Company). Röntgen, an immensely gifted and far-sighted man, was well ahead of his time. He believed in steam passionately; long before Samuel Cunard got his company going, Röntgen was planning and dreaming of regular steamship service across the Atlantic. In 1839, Röntgen drafted a memorandum proposing immediate establishment of the Nederlandsche Stoomvaart Maatschappij op Noord-Amerika (Netherlands Steamship Company to North America). He estimated that it would require Dfl. 1,200,000 (equivalent in 1839 to about £100,000) to construct a steamship of 2000 tons gross register, the size needed for regular Rotterdam-to-New-York service. A shortage of money and a shortage of imagination — coupled with a lack of Dutch confidence in steam engines as a means of propulsion for oceangoing ships — doomed Röntgen's plan to failure in 1839.

But Röntgen persisted, and so did men such as Marten Mees, Dr. A. Plate, F. Jzn and Jhr. Otto Reuchlin, all urging the Netherlands to enter the transatlantic steamship race. Pamphlets were published, fierce arguments were exchanged between shipping companies and Dutch ports and, finally, in 1872, more than a quarter of a century after Röntgen launched his dream, the dream became reality. On October 15, 1872, the *Rotterdam* made her maiden voyage; she was a steamship with auxiliary sailing power of 1700 tons gross register and a 1300 horsepower compound engine. The ship sailed from Rotterdam with ten cabin passengers, sixty tweendeck emigrants and 800 tons of freight. The *Rotterdam* stopped in Plymouth to replenish her supplies, then, in the space of two weeks, crossed the Atlantic, arriving at the port of New York on November 5, 1872.

Once the Dutch were in the field, they wasted no time expanding. Before the end of 1872, the *Rotterdam* had a sister ship, the *Maas*, later called the *Maasdam*. Monthly service to New York became a reality. The harbor at Rotterdam was opened to the largest seagoing vessels, thanks to the construction of the New Waterway, which had been planned by a young engineer named Pieter Caland. Financial support from banks and from W. A. Scholten, an industrialist from Groningen, enabled the company to expand, and quickly the original limited partnership of Plate, Reuchlin & Co., founded in February, 1871, turned into the Nederlandsche-Amerikaansche Stoomvaart Maatschappij (Netherlands-American Steamship Company), a limited liability company with enough capital to build ships.

In 1874, the *Rotterdam* and the *Maas* were joined in the NASM fleet by two new ships: The *P. Caland* and the *W. A. Scholten*, honoring two of the men who made the fleet possible. The new ships were of 2500 tons gross register, and they could carry fifty cabin passengers, six hundred steerages and 3000 tons of freight. The new ships were faster than their predecessors, too; they cut the crossing time from Plymouth to New York by two days, from fourteen days, six hours to twelve days, four hours, and the crossing time from New York to Plymouth a day and a half, from thirteen days to eleven days, thirteen hours. People could envision the day when the crossing would take only a week.

The years passed quickly in the age of steam, filled with ups and downs, prosperity and crises. An economic slump in the United States in 1873 resulted in lower freight rates for grain in 1874. But still the Dutch fleet expanded. The *San Marco* was acquired, 2236 tons gross register, her name changed to the *Schiedam*. The first *Amsterdam*, 2950 tons gross register, was built in 1891. The *Edam* and the *Leerdam* were added to the fleet. Between 1880 and 1890, the Dutch fleet suffered severe setbacks. The *Edam* was wrecked, the *Rotterdam* stranded and lost, the *Amsterdam* stranded and lost, the *Maasdam* aflame and lost, the *Leerdam* sunk, the *W. A. Scholten* sunk after colliding with the s.s. *Rosa Mary* off Dover. More than 100 of the ship's company of the *Scholten* and four of the ship's officers died in the disaster.

Many years later, the Dutch poet Jan Prins wrote of that unhappy time in his poem, "Rotterdam:"

There was the fleet from every region,
the clipper and the barkantine,
the three-master, her rigging heavenward,
and the ore-carrier, full and wide and heavy,
the Lloyd fleet with names of provinces,
all eleven of them if I'm not mistaken,
the Caland and the Lady Tyler,
the Scholten long since lost.
There they were, ready for every
distant land, each in her own splendor.
It is as if I can still hear their voices,
Sounding a farewell in the winter night.

The Atlantic grew more and more crowded. By 1885, twelve major steamship lines offered service between Europe and New York: Cunard Line, White Star Line, American Line, Allan Line, Red Star Line, Hamburg-American Line, French Line, Norddeutscher Lloyd, Thingvalla Line, Anchor Line, Atlantic Transport Line and the NASM, eventually to become the Holland America Line. The competition for business was cut-throat fierce. Briefly, steerage passengers could cross the Atlantic from Hamburg for as little as seven dollars a person. Before they ruined themselves with competition, the steamship companies got together and agreed to regulate their rates, allowing for a fair profit and a fair price.

After a quarter of a century of slow, troubled growth, the Holland America Line, at the turn of the century, could look back on a total of 1300 voyages across the Atlantic, its ships having carried more than 90,000 cabin passengers, 400,000 steerages and five million tons of freight. Then the first *Statendam,* a magnificent ship of 10,000 tons gross register, was commissioned. By the time it reached the age of fifty, the Holland America Line had weathered World War I. The *Statendam II,* 32,000 tons gross register, had been chartered by the Allies and had sailed under the name *Justicia;* she had been sunk by German torpedoes. As compensation from the British government, the HAL received 60,000 tons of steel; from that steel, a fleet of freighters emerged.

There was a temporary boom in shipbuilding after World War I, but soon a surplus tonnage developed. Work on the *Statendam III* had to be delayed; the ship was not commissioned until April, 1929, just in time to absorb the shock waves of the Depression.

The Depression hit the shipping industry with all the fury of a North Atlantic storm. Between the mid-1920s and the late-1930s, the shareholders in shipping companies had to get along with almost no dividends. The White Star Line, a proud British fleet, went under in 1934, merged into the Cunard Line. Rumors spread that the Holland America Line, too, was doomed.

The reports of the death of the HAL were premature. But the line definitely suffered. Regular services were drastically curtailed. In 1932, the *Nieuw Amsterdam I* disappeared into a shipbreaker's yard in Japan. In 1933, the line sold all ships acquired before 1920, with the sole exception of the *Rotterdam.* The *Vechtdyk* passed into the hands of a Greek ship-owner for merely Dfl. 77,000 (roughly about 30,800 dollars at that time). The *Vechtdyk* had been in Dutch service for only thirteen years.

But at least one encouraging development brightened those dark years. With the help of a substantial credit from the Dutch government, plus its own dwindling resources, the HAL began work on the second *Nieuw Amsterdam,* to be built on the slipway of the Rotterdamsche Droogdok Maatschappij.

On April 10, 1937, Queen Wilhelmina launched the new *Nieuw Amsterdam,* and as the ship slipped into the sea, it seemed to symbolize a new era, restoring the faith of the whole Dutch nation in shipping. Tens of thousands of people turned out to watch the launching. Queen Wilhelmina raised her glass and offered a toast: "To the common good and the safe journey of the new ship, the *Nieuw Amsterdam,*

I propose this toast." Minister Gelissen added his comment: "God grant that this first happy launching of the flagship of the Dutch merchant navy may be a good omen, signaling a prosperous journey into the future. May the *Nieuw Amsterdam* carry the Dutch tricolor wide and long across the seas for the glory and the benefit of our beloved country."

But once again the world was sailing into terrible times. In Spain, a bloody civil war raged. In Germany, Adolf Hitler spread his gospel of a master race. In Italy, Benito Mussolini drew his people into war with Haile Selassie's Ethiopia. Suddenly, for the second time in a quarter of a century, beautiful liners were transformed into sturdy troopships. Once again, the luxury ships, carrying soldiers to combat, carrying citizens to safety, were the targets for submarines.

The end of World War II meant the end of torpedoes. But it also meant the beginning of the end for the transatlantic steamship, for the entire concept that the best way to cross the

Menu illustration
by Piet van der Hem

ocean is by ship. With the end of the war, steam engines gave way to turbines and mighty diesel engines; the ships were larger, faster and sleeker, but they were losing their earlier purpose. The bridge across the ocean was turning into an aerial bridge, a route for winged giants that could even then carry almost one hundred passengers from Europe to America in less than a full day.

And yet the liner was not heading for extinction. It was heading for a new life, a new purpose, a purpose that would be handsomely served by the *Nieuw Amsterdam*, the *Statendam*, the *Rotterdam*, the *Volendam*, the *Veendam*, the *Prinsendam* and such sleek new competitors as the *Leonardo da Vinci*. The age of the cruise was approaching, the age when a floating island could offer relaxation, peace and calm, an oasis in a roaring jet age.

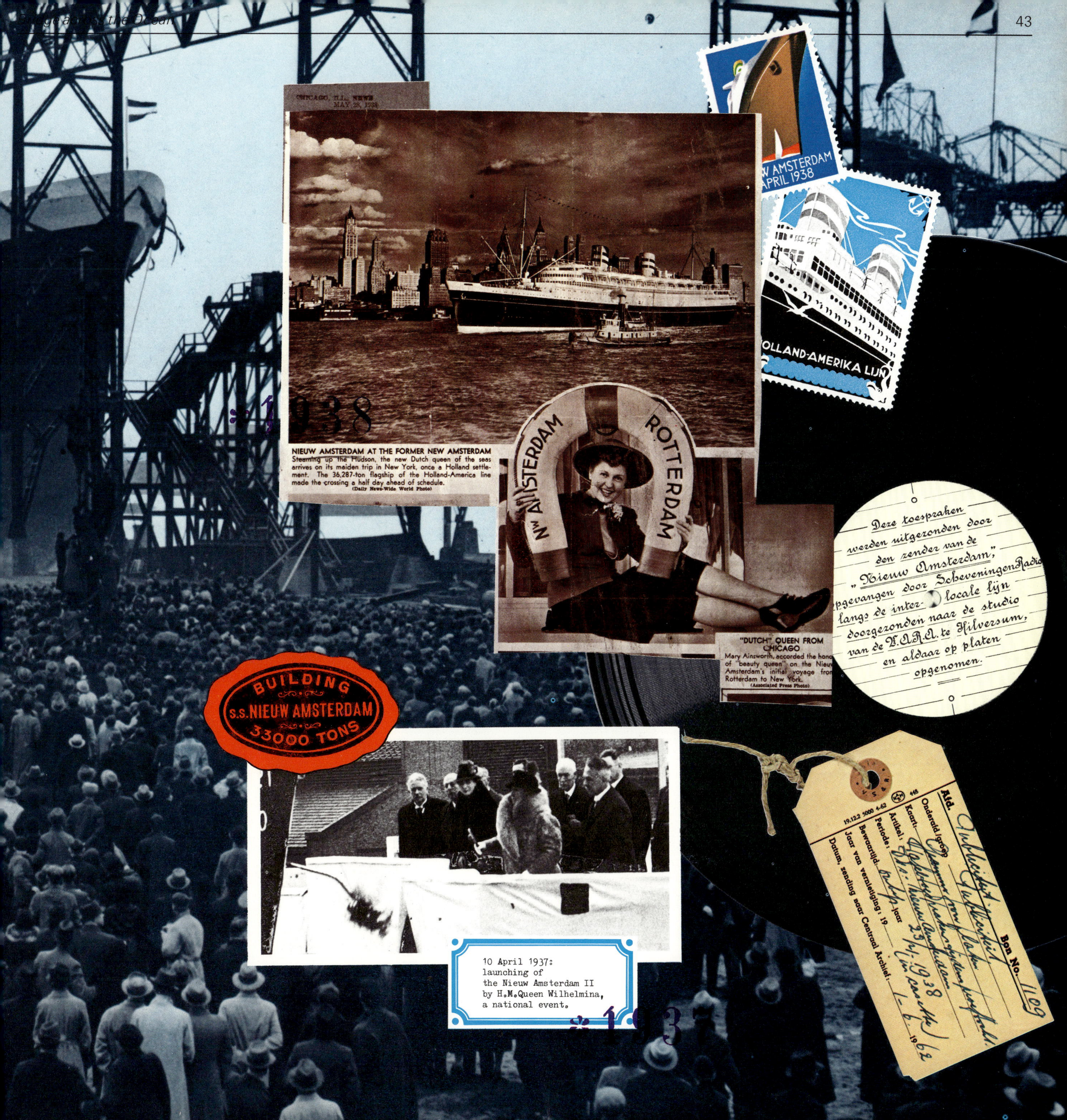

CHICAGO, ILL. NEWS
MAY 28, 1938
1938
NIEUW AMSTERDAM AT THE FORMER NEW AMSTERDAM
Steaming up the Hudson, the new Dutch queen of the seas arrives on its maiden trip in New York, once a Holland settlement. The 36,287-ton flagship of the Holland-America line made the crossing a half day ahead of schedule.
(Daily News-Wide World Photo)
NEW AMSTERDAM
APRIL 1938
HOLLAND-AMERIKA LIJN
Nw AMSTERDAM
ROTTERDAM
"DUTCH" QUEEN FROM CHICAGO
Mary Ainsworth, accorded the hono of "beauty queen" on the Nieuw Amsterdam's initial voyage fro Rotterdam to New York.
(Associated Press Photo)
Deze toespraken werden uitgezonden door den zender van de "Nieuw Amsterdam," opgevangen door Scheveningen Radio langs de inter- locale lijn doorgezonden naar de studio van de V.A.R.A. te Hilversum, en aldaar op platen opgenomen.
BUILDING
S.S. NIEUW AMSTERDAM
33000 TONS
Afd.
Onderafd./groep
Kaart
Artikel
Periode
Bewaartijd
Jaar van vernietiging: 19
Datum. zending naar Centraal Archief.
Bon No.
1937

10 April 1937:
launching of
the Nieuw Amsterdam II
by H.M.Queen Wilhelmina,
a national event.

NIEUW AMSTERDAM

s.s. Nieuw Amsterdam II / design Alphons Dullaart / 1949 / poster deta

Chicago piano. The phrase keeps running through my mind. It's a catchy phrase, short and hard, and I guess it summarizes for me what happens to the shipping industry, to luxury liners, when nations decide to go to war.

During my conversations aboard the s.s. *Nieuw Amsterdam,* several persons offered their impressions of the impact of war. ''There was a shortage of sugar in America,'' said John Last, the box manufacturer from New Jersey. ''Cargo space had to be utilized to carry supplies to the fronts in Europe and the Pacific.''

An elderly couple, Jozef and Miriam Litschky, had a very personal and poignant view. ''Our son, David,'' they told me, as we cruised through the Caribbean, ''returned from the European invasion aboard this ship. He came home in 1945, wounded but alive. For years now, he has been living with his wife and children in Israel.''

But it was a Dutchman, Cor Stapel, who really captured my imagination. ''Chicago piano,'' he said. ''That was the troops' nickname for the massive twelve-barrel anti-aircraft guns installed on the top deck of the *Nieuw Amsterdam* during World War II.''

Chicago piano. Submarine warfare. Submarines in the Caribbean and off the coast of South America.

''In those years, we forgot that gales and hurricanes existed,'' said Stapel, once the purser aboard the *Nieuw Amsterdam,* now the buyer for the Holland America Line on Pier 40 in New York. ''We had other worries. We carried 8000 soldiers. Once, when we spotted an unfamiliar ship, all 8000 soldiers — at least it seemed that way — rushed to starboard. The ship almost capsized. Captain Barendse had to issue a standing order that whenever we spotted something on the sea, the troops had to go to their quarters immediately. We called that leveling out.

''We were often scared. Just imagine what could have happened if 8000 soldiers ever panicked. With all the portholes blacked out, without any lights, we zigzagged our way across the Atlantic. It stank on board. Between New York and Glasgow, we almost never had a strong drink.

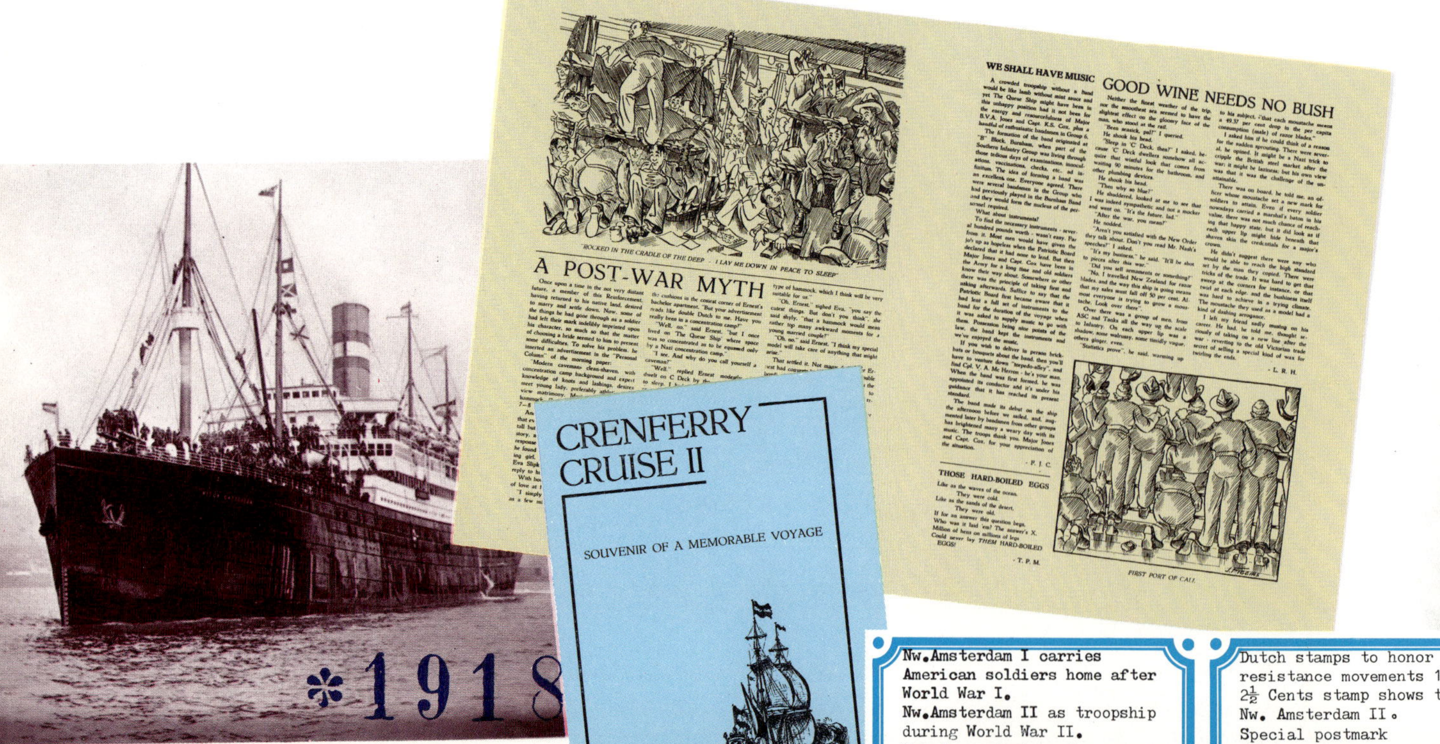

5 c
HR. MS. DE RUYTER
NEDERLAND
NEDERLAND
1½ c
NEDERLAND
2½ CENT 2½
S.S. NIEUW AMSTERDAM
Rotterdam - New York
October 29th 1947
FIRST POSTWAR VOYAGE
S.S. NIEUW AMSTERDAM
HOLLAND-AMERICA LINE
OCEAN POST

We had to keep our eyes open, our minds alert. But as soon as we reached Glasgow, it was different. Even the captain told the agents and the representatives, 'If you want to talk to the officers, you'll have to be quick!' Then the corks flew."

The two World Wars were a terrible time on land. They were a terrible time on sea, too. During World War I, Holland was theoretically neutral; somebody forgot to tell the German torpedoes.

In August, 1914, the original *Nieuw Amsterdam*, under the command of Captain Jan Baron, was pressed into service to carry home a full shipload of American tourists anxious to get home from Europe as fast as possible. The British and French liners had stopped running. The *Nieuw Amsterdam* sailed out of Rotterdam with 597 first-class passengers, 389 second-class and 676 third-class. The tables in the dining room were filled all day long, one sitting after another. When the last sitting finished breakfast, it was time for the first sitting to eat lunch; the cycle was repeated from lunch to dinner.

The conditions could not have been more trying, yet the crew did such a masterful job that the passengers spontaneously decided to have a commemorative tablet presented to the s.s. *Nieuw Amsterdam*.

Three Dutch seamen lost their lives when the s.s. *Ryndam* was torpedoed in 1916. The most precious possession of the HAL, the *Rotterdam*, was laid up that year for the duration of the war. But the heaviest loss in the war was the sinking of the second *Statendam*; the ship was chartered by the British government and launched in Belfast as the troopship *Justicia*.

On July 25, 1918, at three in the afternoon, the *Justicia* was attacked by German U-boats off the coast of Ireland. One hit was scored by a torpedo, but still the ship remained afloat, refusing to accept an early end. British destroyers rushed to the scene and took the crippled ship in tow. But the U-boats followed, and before the destroyers could tow the *Justicia* to safety, a well-placed torpedo finished off the proud 35,000-ton ship. She had never sailed for the Holland America Line.

Yet, financially, the HAL did well during World War I. HAL shares which had slipped into foreign hands when the International Mercantile Marine Corporation was formed by the American Morgan Trust in 1902 could even be bought back. Considerable reserves for new building could be set aside. At the end of the war, the HAL had twenty-three ships in shape for Atlantic passenger and freight service.

World War II was much more harsh. The war came to the Netherlands on May 10, 1940. It hit at three-thirty in the morning, and it hit like a cyclone. German troops invaded the country. Parachute troops floated down around Rotterdam. The city was heavily bombed. The old port bled from a thousand wounds. In the harbor, thick clouds of smoke rose from the burning *Statendam III* and the *Boschdyk*, hit by artillery fire. Practically all the sheds of the HAL on the Wilhelmina Quay were destroyed. The Dutch shipping industry was crippled, almost exterminated. Yet out at sea there were 1867 men and women aboard sixteen ships. They had escaped the German onslaught, and throughout the war, these men, women and ships made their contributions to the victory of the free world.

(Continued on Next

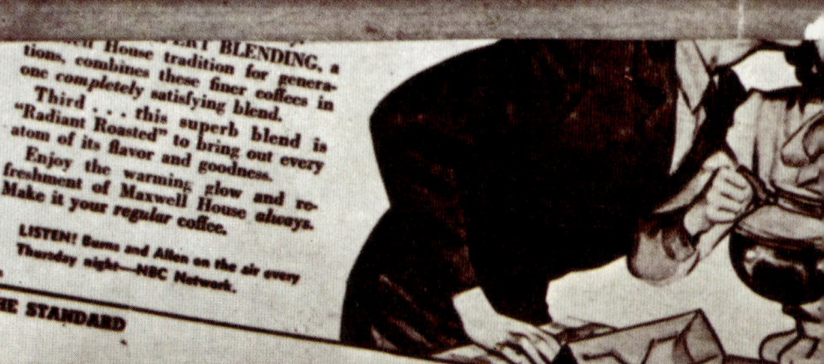

BOATDRILL was held every morning. With war over, chief danger was from fire. Smoking is allowed only on open decks and in the lounges.

BRITISH "NAVY SHOW" entertains troops. Risqué humor, typical of British shows, made troops self-conscious with Canadian service-women in audience.

Troopship *(Continued)*

FIRST GLIMPSE OF CANADA, as Air Force officer points out headland. Hours before expected arrival at Halifax, passengers lined the rails.

DANGER ZONE past, Corp. Victor Chicione of Sherbrooke, Que., uses lifebelt to write letters.

LIFE JACKETS were carried for first 24 hours. On deck are (left) LAWs Maureen Stephenson and Norma Johnson, both of Edmonton.

TWO SISTERS, Corp. Muriel and Pte. Audrey Scott, CWAC, of Winnipeg. Overseas six years, they were on holiday in England when war broke out.

LOUNGES were crowded from morning till night. Here officers play chess. Gambling is taboo but went on everywhere in ship.

LIKE MANY returning Canadians, CSO Oliver Martin of Winnipeg wonders how family will react to new moustache acquired in Europe.

CARRYING over 8,000 troops, the Nieuw Amsterdam still offered plenty of deckspace for walking.

Troopship *(Concluded)*

such messy jobs as the French Pasteur. And she's modern, has every latest gadget including a loghorn in the bow which can be heard 22 miles ahead but is barely audible on rear decks.

On the crossing, the troops divided their time between writing letters, strolling the decks, playing cards, listening to concerts several times a day, and reading "Forever Amber."

Hours before we reached Halifax, the men lined the ship's rails straining their eyes for the first glimpse of Canada. When it came, they excitedly pointed it out to their friends. A corvette came out, blowing its siren and practically tipping over while doing a U-turn around our stern.

As we steamed into Halifax Harbor, a beflagged little boat came out with a band playing on her deck, CWAC's waving, and WELCOME HOME across her side. Factory hooters screamed. A fireboat crossed our bows with all hoses playing.

So many people crowded on the port side as the ship edged into the pier that over the loud speaker came the warning: "If half of you don't move to the starboard side you'll all be sent below decks." Nobody took any notice and the pilot got her along side safely, though by that time crossing her decks was like scaling a steep ramp.

As we watched the cheering families down on the pier I noticed a sergeant next to me. He was a stockily-built, leathery-laced tough-looking customer. He wiped his wet cheeks with the back of his hand and said "This salt spray sure makes your eyes water, doesn't it."

Within Holland, a man named Captain Filippo performed a feat of uncommon bravery. In the face of German restrictions and German threats, Captain Filippo collected money whenever and wherever he could, money to be given to the families of the men and women fighting for freedom on Dutch ships. Captain Filippo brought in a former merchant marine officer, Walraven van Hall, to manage the fund, the outlawed "Seamen's Fund." Walraven van Hall did such a fine job the Germans could not find out where the money was coming from nor how it was being distributed. The Seamen's Fund paid out a total of seven million guilders in allowances, one million of which went to the families of men of the Royal Netherlands Navy. To this day, the Seamen's Fund is considered a prime example of the solidarity that persisted in Holland during the five dark years of German occupation.

The bridge across the Atlantic, across all the seven seas, became, in effect, a tunnel of terror. Prowling submarines were everywhere. In August, 1940, the s.s. *Volendam*, under the command of Captain J. P. Wepster, sailed from Britain to Canada. The *Volendam* was the commodore ship of a convoy of thirty-six ships. On August 30, at eleven o'clock at night, the ship was hit by a torpedo. There were a great many children aboard, children who were being evacuated because of the heavy German air raids. The children were all asleep when the torpedo struck. Yet, in perfect order, the children, women and men abandoned the ship, efficiently and safely. Captain Wepster, who was later killed when the s.s. *Zaandam*, under his command, was torpedoed off the Brazilian coast, gave a written report of the *Volendam* incident: "Everybody remained extremely calm. There was no running around or rushing about, no feeling of panic. The children had gone through several boat drills, and getting them to their boat stations went smoothly. The behavior of the children inspired their elders — or, perhaps, vice-versa. In fact, I have the greatest admiration

TRANSPORT OF AMERICAN SOL

RS PER S.S. "RIJNDAM", ON TERMINATION OF THE WAR

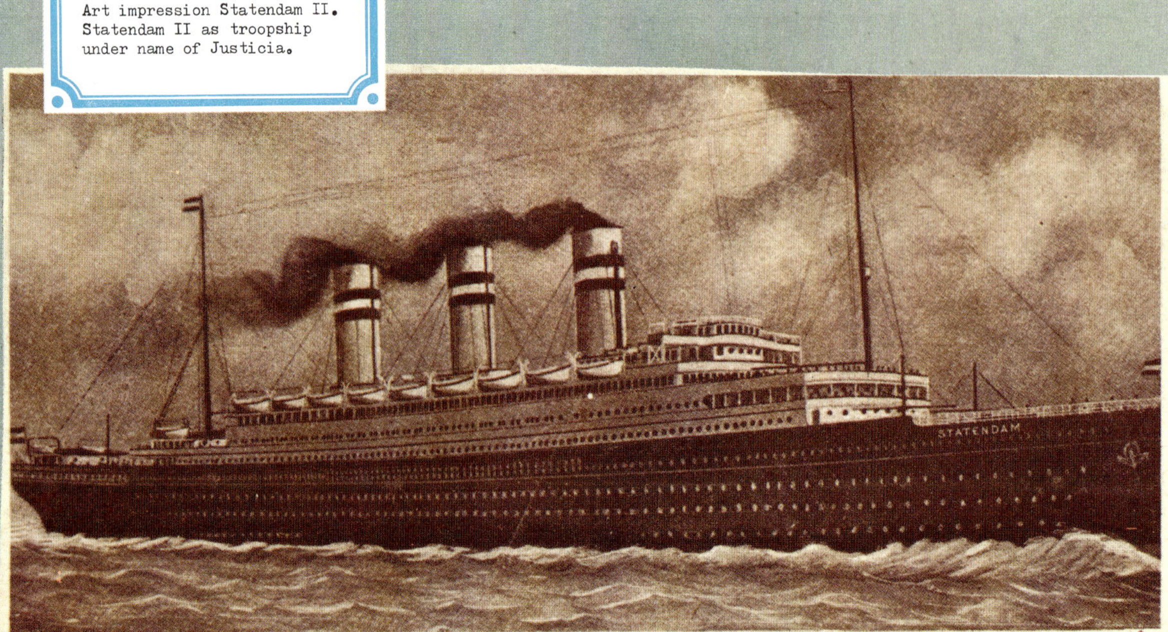

1918

Art impression Statendam II.
Statendam II as troopship
under name of Justicia.

HET S.S. »STATENDAM« GETORPEDEERD. 1918
Het Nederlandsche stoomschip »Statendam« varende onder den naam van »Justitia« werd onlangs ten Noorden van de Iersche kust getorpedeerd. Dit schip werd zooals men weet in het begin van den oorlog door de Engelsche regeering gerequireerd en hoorde oorspronkelijk toe aan de Holland-Amerikalijn. Het mat 32.000 ton en zou het grootste Nederlandsche schip geweest zijn.

for everyone's conduct. Every sailor remained at his post – the engine room staff down below, the crew lowering the life boats, the men checking the condition of the ship – and all did their duty. It was a moving, impressive experience to hear the children singing in the life boats, defying the rough sea. The whole thing seemed more like a perfect exercise than a real happening."

The only casualty was R. Baron, the ship's purser. While getting into his lifeboat, he slipped overboard and drowned.

Chicago piano. Twelve-barrel ack-ack guns. They drowned out the sounds of the gay twenties, the roaring twenties, the days of flower-pot hats, long strings of beads, boas, ostrich feathers and long cigarette holders.

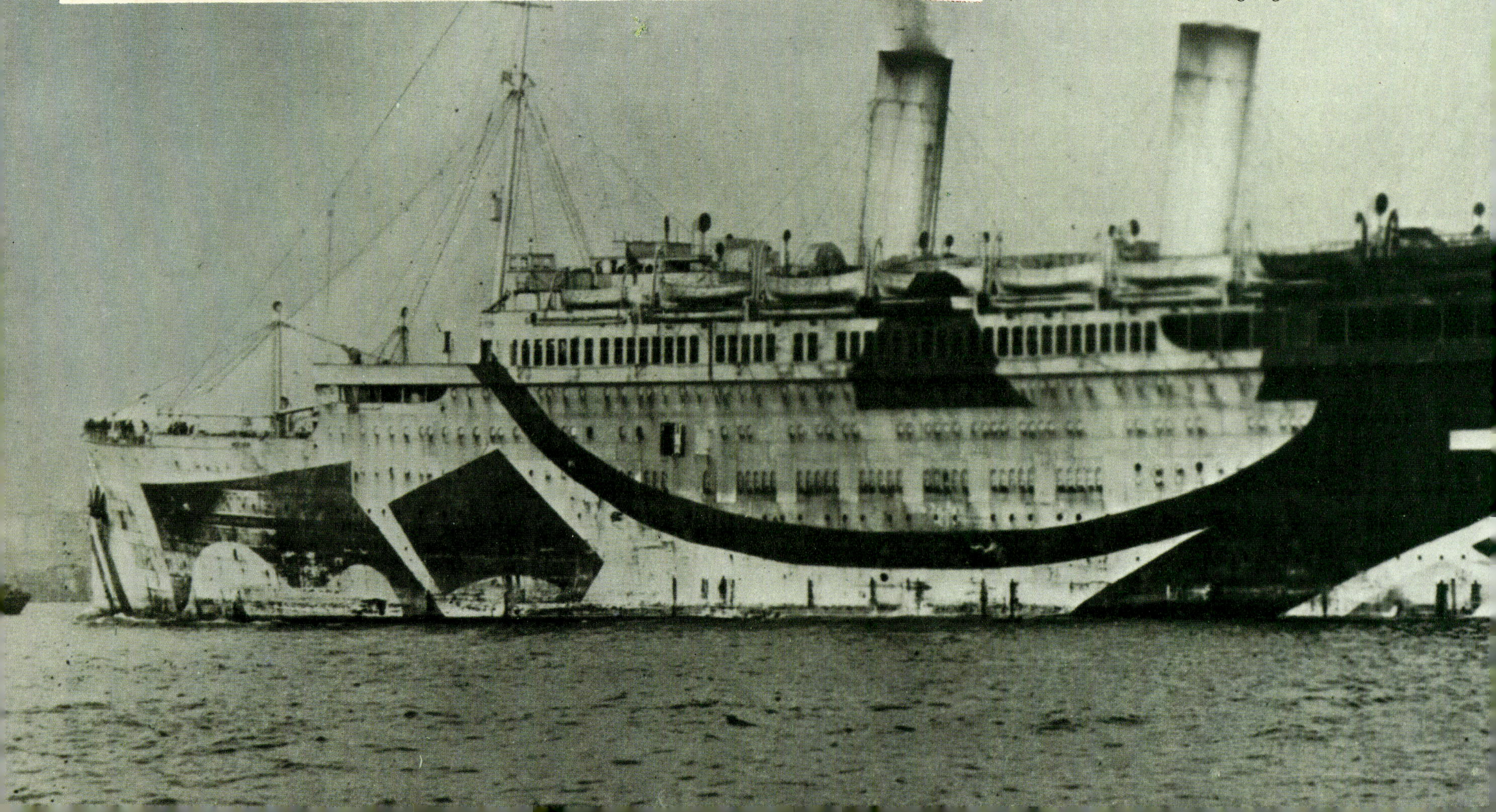

Forgotten in the boom of the ack-ack guns were the years of poverty after the stock market crash. Forgotten was the economic revival triggered by Franklin Roosevelt's New Deal. Forgotten were the popular winter cruises on the *Rotterdam* and similar ships in the years when the average American yearned to be free of Prohibition. Forgotten were the card sharks who booked cruises in order to be able to ply their trade among unsuspecting fellow passengers. Forgotten was the marvelous reception accorded the *Nieuw Amsterdam* when she ended her maiden voyage at the pier in Hoboken, New Jersey, on May 17, 1938. She had made the trip from Rotterdam, under the command of Captain Johannes Bijl, in five days, 23 hours and 45 minutes.

The glamor of the *Nieuw Amsterdam's* first trip back to Europe still lives in yellowed cuttings from the New York newspapers of the day. There were many prominent persons heading East aboard the *Nieuw Amsterdam*: Mary Ainworth, famous as a fashion designer and as a writer of fashion articles under the name of Jane Alden; Spencer Tracy, the actor, and Ina Claire, the actress; Miss Marjorie Shuler, a correspondent for the Christian Science Monitor, who was to leave the ship in Europe and begin a 30,000-mile airplane journey; Paul Gallico, the author; Allan Nevins, the Pulitzer Prize-winning biographer; John V. A. MacMurray, the American ambassador to Turkey; Arthur Brentano, the publisher; I. J. Fox, the furrier, making his sixteenth crossing in twelve years; and Stephen Frankel, the leader of the Metropolitan Opera Company's orchestra. A flower-and-fashion show was held aboard the new ship, and the guests included Roy W. Howard, the president of the Scripps-Howard newspapers, and Basil Harris, the vice-president of the United States Line.

Columnists who covered the sailing seemed to take great delight in describing the furnishing aboard the *Nieuw Amsterdam* — the work of such Dutch artists as Piet Starreveld, Nel Klaassen, Joan Collette, Jaap Sidding, John Raedecker, Hendrik Chabot, Joep Nicolas, professor H. Campendonk, Charles Eyck and Andreas D. Copier, and such Dutch architects as Hendrik T. Wijdeveld, Jan P. L. Hendriks, J. J. P. Oud, Frits Spanjaard and Frits A. Eschausier. The ship was carrying 20,000 silver dishes and coffee- and tea-pots, plus 400,000 pieces of linen; there were three kitchens in operation, and one reporter even recorded the recipe for the dish she was served, the Dutch "kletskoppen":

War. Bombs on Rotterdam.
The Wilhelminakade in ruins.
Statendam III on fire.

*1940

Rotterdam II (enlarged picture stamp). Rotterdam III building in Belfast.

1½ cups brown sugar. 1 teaspoon cinnamon.
2 tablespoons water. 2 cups ground almonds.
¼ cup butter. 1 cup flour.

Mix sugar and water to make a thick paste. Add butter, cinnamon, almonds and flour. Shape in small rounds, about an inch in diameter, on a baking sheet, greased with unsalted fat, at least two inches apart. Bake about 15 minutes in moderate oven (325 degrees F.). Remove from oven, let stand half a minute and lift from baking sheet with a spatula.

Chicago piano. Forgotten in its outburst were the emigrants who headed for America, the Spanish seasonal workers bound for Mexico and Cuba, the Syrians who moved to Mexico. Forgotten, too, was one furious cruise passenger who, during the days of Prohibition, found himself in a cabin that actually had the ship's mast cutting straight through the room. When the passenger had booked passage, he had been told by his travel agent that the round circle shown in the plan of the cabin was a coffee table. He was stunned when the table turned out to be a mast, and he rushed to complain to the ship's manager. Furious, the passenger shouted: "Do you know what your agent told me when I booked this damn ship? He said I'd be surprised!"

The manager gave the perfect answer. "Well, you are, aren't you?" he said. Even the passenger had to laugh. He calmed down and made the best of his unusual accomodations. At the end of the trip, he told the manager, "It was an awful cabin, but a wonderful trip."

There were no wonderful trips during World War II. All through Europe, the lights of the cities were dim. London trembled under heavy air raids. And in New York, thousands of European seamen — driven away from their own shores by German occupation — waited for assignments aboard their requisitioned ships. Some of them had to wait six years to find out the fate of their families back home. On all the fronts of the war, on sea as well as on land, displaced Europeans listened to the song, "Lily Marlene," which echoed their homesickness and their longing for peace.

Rotterdam IV. 24.149 tgr.
One of the biggest ships
in the world. First ship with
promenade deck completely
enclosed by glass.(Illustration from HAL pamphlet.)

Deck lay-out Rotterdam IV.
Capacity: 532 first-class,
555 second-class,
2,230 third-class passengers.

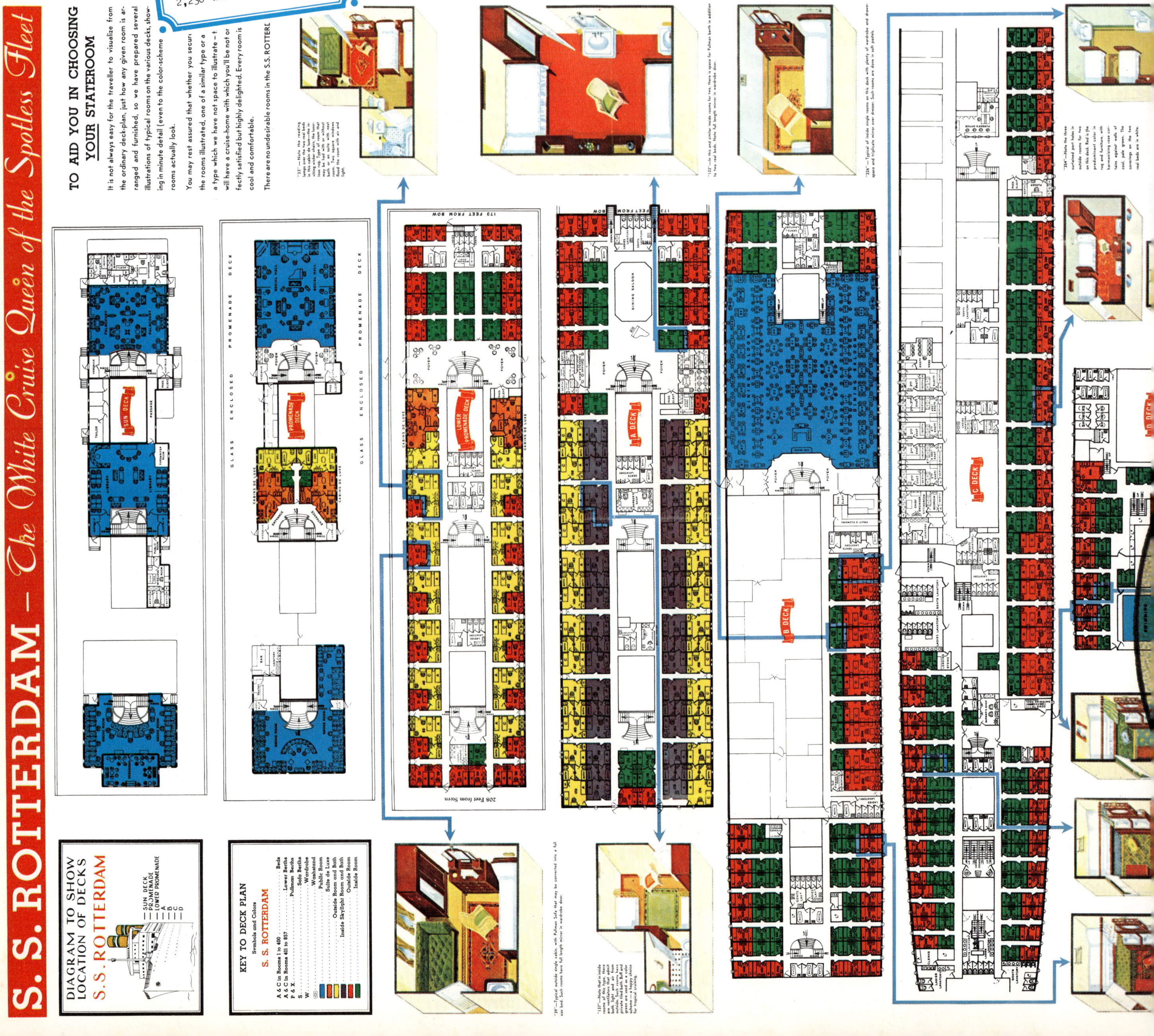

TO AID YOU IN CHOOSING YOUR STATEROOM

It is not always easy for the traveller to visualize from the ordinary deck-plan, just how any given room is arranged and furnished, so we have prepared several illustrations of typical rooms on the various decks, showing in minute detail (even to the color-scheme) how the rooms actually look.

You may rest assured that whether you secure the rooms illustrated, one of a similar type or a a type which we have not space to illustrate — t will have a cruise-home with which you'll be not or fectly satisfied but highly delighted. Every room is cool and comfortable.

There are no undesirable rooms in the S.S. ROTTERI

DIAGRAM TO SHOW
LOCATION OF DECKS
S.S. ROTTERDAM

SUN DECK
PROMENADE
LOWER PROMENADE
A
B
C
D

KEY TO DECK PLAN

Symbols and Colors

S. S. ROTTERDAM

A & C in Rooms 1 to 400 . . . . Beds
A & C in Rooms 401 to 857 . . . . Lower Berths
P & X . . . . Pullman Berths
S . . . . Sofa Berths
W . . . . Wardrobe
. . . . Washstand
. . . . Public Room
. . . . Suite de Luxe
. . . . Outside Room and Bath
. . . . Inside Skylight Room and Bath
. . . . Outside Room
. . . . Inside Room

Chicago piano. Captain Cornelis Visser never heard the sound of the ack-ack guns. On May 10, 1940, when the Germans swept into The Netherlands, he was berthed in Rotterdam with the *Damsterdyk*. ''I didn't manage to get away,'' Captain Visser says. ''I went back to the nautical training college for a while. Then I got a job at the Vegetable and Fruit Board at The Hague. But once the great railway strike in the Netherlands began, I could no longer travel from Rotterdam to The Hague. During the hunger-winter of 1944—45, I managed the central people's kitchen in Rotterdam. You have no idea of the misery we faced there. Starvation. Disease. People dying in the streets.''

Captain Visser suffered doubly — from the misery within the Netherlands and from the misery of not being at sea, helping the fight for freedom. He was a seaman for forty-one years, and when he retired in 1956, he was captain of the *Nieuw Amsterdam*. To him, the Dutch slogan dating back to the seventeenth century —

HOLLAND-AMERICA LINE

Menu/postcard illustrations:
third-class cabin and
smoking room Rotterdam III.
Insets: First-class cabin
and third-class toilet
Rotterdam IV.

''Sailing, if need be, with burning sails through hell'' — had always meant a great deal. He loved the sea from childhood, and in 1957, after his retirement from the Holland America Line, he sailed from Germany to America aboard a 117-foot yacht. Now he lives in San Clemente, California, in a home for the aged; he is in his late seventies, but from his apartment he can glimpse the ocean, and when he sees that the *Moerdyk* or the *Grotedyk* is coming into Los Angeles, he hurries to the docks to renew old acquaintances and recount old stories. ''Someday,'' he says, ''I would like to cross the Atlantic once more in a small boat.''

Chicago piano. First Mate Pieter van Beelen — like Captain Visser — did not spend much of World War II where he wanted to be. ''I was first officer on the *Pennland*,'' Pieter van Beelen says, ''and on April 25, 1941, fifty miles from Athens, we were bombed by German aircraft. We were on our way to evacuate Australian troops from Greece. One bomb exploded in the engine room. Four people were dead, many were injured.

I went downstairs, and the situation was hopeless. We had to abandon ship. We took to the lifeboats, and a British destroyer picked us up."

For three days, Pieter van Beelen stayed on the island of Crete, living in an olive orchard. Then German parachutists invaded Crete. With 2000 troops and 600 Italian prisoners of war, Pieter van Beelen escaped aboard a small freighter to Egypt. (The freighter carried only two lifeboats, not quite enough considering the passenger list.) Pieter van Beelen then traveled from Cairo to Suez by train, from Suez to Cape Town on a British troopship, from Cape Town to New York by cruise ship. In New York, he was kept ashore, handling administrative details concerning troopships. Even after the war ended, he stayed ashore, working for the HAL on Pier 40. "For twenty-two years," he says, "from 1941 till I retired in 1963, I longed to be at sea. Do you realize how it hurts to stay ashore when you were born at Noordwijk on the sea?"

In New York, during the war, Pieter van Beelen's job was to see that every ship was provided with a crew. "Sometimes, men had just escaped being killed when their ship was torpedoed," he says, "and we had to send them back to sea again. Every ship needed a crew. Every convoy needed all its ships. Sometimes I brought in people from Martinique just to keep the ships going."

Occasionally, Pieter van Beelen visited injured seamen in New York hospitals. Sometimes he brought them brief messages from their families in Europe, messages carried by the Red Cross through Portugal. "I was a member of the committee led by Leo van Münching, the importer of Heineken's beer in New York (and a former HAL employee)," says van Beelen. "He did a lot for those injured men, trying to help them through their homesickness, their feeling of helplessness in regard to their families in Europe. The men could convalesce at a lovely home on Long Island; women came by for dances. The people in New York had a fantastic attitude. They did everything they could to make life more bearable, more enjoyable for those thousands of seamen separated from their homes."

Pieter van Beelen had one very special assignment during World War II. He was sent to pick up Cornelis van der Vlot in Florida and bring him to New York. Cornelis van der Vlot was one of three shipwrecked sailors who survived for 83 days aboard a raft in the Atlantic. "He was just skin and bones when I saw him for the first time." Pieter van Beelen recalls. "He was a very humble person. When I told him that he was expected by the Royal Family in Canada, he began to cry."

The story of Cornelis van der Vlot, and of Nico Hoogendam and an American, Basil Izzi, is one of the epics of the sea. They were among 132 seamen who went down with the *Zaandam* off Recife, Brazil; Cornelis van der Vlot, a fireman aboard the ship, was thirty-seven years old; Hoogendam was seventeen, and Izzi twenty. Originally, there were five people aboard the raft, and they had enough food and drinking water to last sixteen days. One of the five, George Beasley, an American, died on the 66th day; another American, James Maddox, died eleven days later. Six days after that, the three survivors were rescued; they had been adrift on the open sea, unprotected, for a longer period than any other men in history.

"Drinking water was their greatest problem," says Pieter van Beelen. "Cornelis was very ingenious. He caught fish through a hole in the raft. He wrung them out and caught the moisture from the fish. It was not salty, and it was potable."

Of the three survivors, Cornelis van der Vlot was the only one who could stand up at all when they were finally rescued. The other two had to be carried off the raft. "After a few weeks in New York recuperating," says Pieter van Beelen, "Cornelis felt like his old self. He went right back to sea. He was an excellent worker."

Chicago piano. Six ships of the Holland America fleet were sunk during World War II: *Pennland, Zaandam, Breedyk, Beemsterdyk, Bilderdyk* and *Maasdam.* Ten ships survived: *Volendam, Delftdyk, Sloterdyk, Sommelsdyk, Blommersdyk, Westerdam, Leerdam, Noordam, Edam* and the *Nieuw Amsterdam.* The *Nieuw Amsterdam* alone — the "Dutchman's favorite," the most popular of all troopships, the flagship of the HAL and the largest ship of the Dutch

Contrasts:
First-class dining room
Rotterdam III
(pamphlet illustration),
third-class dining room
Rotterdam IV.

DINING-SALOON

merchant navy — steamed half a million miles
during the war and carried 400,000 soldiers
to the fronts in the Pacific and in Europe.
Somewhere on the ship, a few names which
sailors carved in the ship's timber are said to
have been preserved.

Jacob van den Berg, a ship's engineer
aboard the wartime *Nieuw Amsterdam,*
remembers transporting prisoners of war from
North Africa to the United States. ''Sometimes it
was a pretty unpleasant sight,'' he says, ''seeing
those chaps behind barbed wire. After all, they
were human beings, too, and all of a sudden,
they were being shipped thousands of miles to
an uncertain future.''

Cor Stapel — the man who told me
about Chicago piano — was aboard the
Westernland when the war broke out. ''Our first
taste of violence came on a Sunday morning,''
says Stapel, who later sailed on the *Nieuw
Amsterdam*. ''We were riding at anchor in
Falmouth Bay, England, next to a crippled
destroyer. Suddenly, we were startled by a
tremendous noise. Gunfire. A Stuka over the
bay. In no time, two trawlers were aflame.

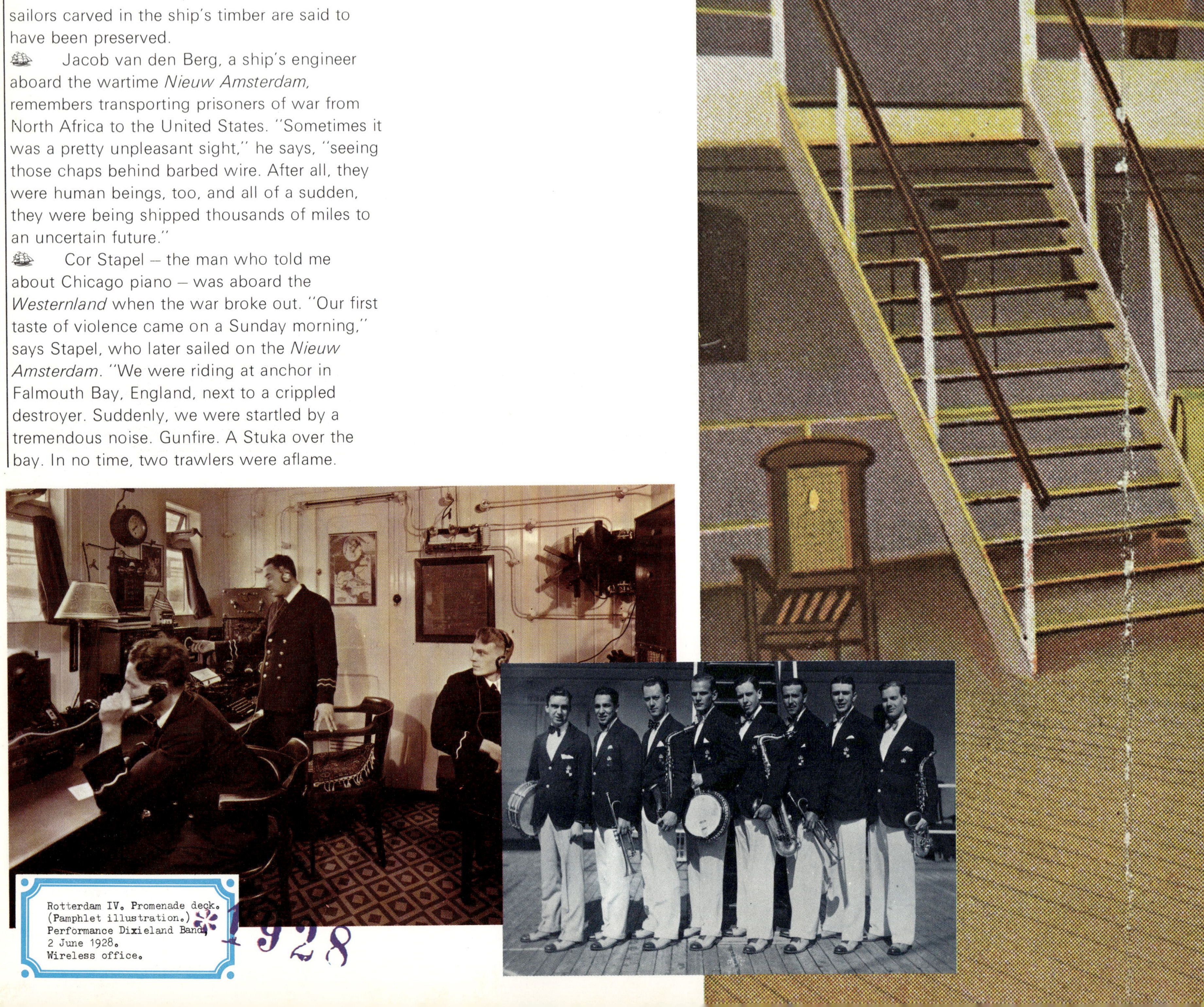

Rotterdam IV. Promenade deck.
(Pamphlet illustration.)
Performance Dixieland Band.
2 June 1928.
Wireless office.

"There were some lighter moments. We had hundreds of stranded Dutch marines on board, and, naturally, we fed them. Those boys were penniless. But we knew how much they would have loved a beer. I went to Captain Pieter Lagaay and said, 'What can we do about that?' And the captain said, 'Just let them sign a voucher.' Those boys signed vouchers. They sure did. With such names as Maarten Tromp, Piet Hein, Michiel de Ruyter…" The names came straight out of Dutch maritime history.

On one voyage early in the war, the *Westernland* served as the command ship for General Charles de Gaulle; the ship carried 1200 Free French soldiers. It was in an armada off Dakar in North Africa. The plan was to get the Petain troops of the local garrison to surrender the town to de Gaulle. The plan didn't work. A grandson of Field Marshal Foch went toward shore in the speedy motor launch of the *Westernland*, flying a white flag. The boat was met with a hail of bullets.

Heavy fire from the French battleship *Richelieu*, which was lying half-sunk in the harbor, was directed at the armada. The British battleship *Resolute* received a hit from a submarine which had slipped out of the harbor. The crew of the *Westernland* offered to try to take the Free French troops ashore in lifeboats for an attack upon the garrison, but General de Gaulle decided the situation was hopeless. The

Two ships, two interiors. Lounge Rotterdam III, satin, rosewood, tiles from Rozenburg Pottery, The Hague. Palm Court and lounge Rotterdam IV. After the refit with swimming pool.

Art impression dining room Nieuw Amsterdam II. Famous Dutch artists enhance the ship.

Westernland disembarked the Free French troops in Freetown, and the general and his staff went back to the relative safety of England.

Cor Stapel recalls that the Free French troops had plenty of money. "They came from Norway," he says, "and they had their pockets full of English pounds. They did nothing but play and drink. We sold them beer by the quart bottle. A mess attendant crammed the pounds sterling into a large case. When we were cleaning up the ship one day, someone accidentally put the case out on deck, unmarked and unguarded. We went looking for it, and found a soldier sitting on top of it. He had no idea what he was resting on. He didn't know that he could have had a fortune just by opening the case."

After Dakar, Cor Stapel, Captain Lagaay and the rest of the crew of the *Westernland* went to Port Sudan. There, they picked up a contingent of black French army-workers. "Those chaps came straight from the bush," Stapel says. "They had never worn any shoes in their lives. They staggered down the gangway on all fours when they were met at their destination by a military band and a committee of colonels. It was a rather strange sight."

The *Westernland* later went back and forth between Suez and Bombay, bringing Indian troops to Field Marshal Montgomery and ferrying prisoners of war back to India. At one time, the ship carried a distinguished prisoner of war, the long-bearded Italian general, Annibale "Electric Whiskers" Bergonzoli. Stapel still remembers the scorching heat on the coal burning ship. "Temperatures reached up to 130 degrees F.," he says. "Not one member of the crew was without ulcers. We had outbreaks of German measles. Men literally died on watch duty. I saw a man one day leaning like a stone image against his bunk. When we touched him, he just fell over. Dead.

"And yet, despite all this, the *Westernland* was a lucky ship. Time after time, she had a fortunate escape. Once we were booked for Crete to evacuate troops, but our coal supplies were too low. The *Pennland* took our place, and she was bombed. Another time,

in the Bay of Suez, we were lying next to the British ship *Georgic*. The Germans bombed the bay, and the *Georgic* burst into flames. The *Westernland* didn't even have a scratch. "We were even able to lower our boats and save people from the *Georgic*. Many women and children. It puzzles me right up to this day how we managed to escape. They must have seen us. Our ship was blacked out, but how can you hide a shower of sparks from the funnel?"

The *Blommersdyk* was another gallant ship that survived. Jacob van den Berg spent three war years aboard her. "How that ship did her utmost," he says. "With a speed of only ten knots, we trudged through dangerous waters. The Red Sea. Suez. South Africa. The Atlantic. The food was often terrible, a kind of dahlia tubers with rice. On deck, our big weapon was a 1914 gun. In Freetown, in the scorching African heat, we were taught to shoot with that thing."

Chicago piano. Lily Marlene. Homesickness. Gay cruises to the West Indies were only faded memories. It was hard to believe that it was only in 1938 that F. R. Wierdsma, the general manager of the HAL in New York, had delivered a glowingly optimistic speech aboard the new *Nieuw Amsterdam*: "The *Rotterdam* is leaving with 600 passengers for an eleven-day cruise to Bermuda, Nassau and Havana. That's an increase of fifty per cent in number of passengers over last year. Our whole line shows a twenty-five per cent increase in traffic. Three hundred passengers have already booked space on the *Veendam*, which will sail for thirty days to Curaçao, La Guayra and San Juan. Cruises have a future."

The cruises certainly did have a future, but Wierdsma couldn't have known then that the future would have to wait. Before the Caribbean could be explored leisurely by tourists, the devilish job of war had to be done. "Sailing, if need be, with burning sails through hell." In October, 1938, New York society columns heralded the arrival of Henry Cabot Lodge, Thomas Mann and Secretary of State Sumner Welles aboard the *Nieuw Amsterdam*; in the next few months, Secretary of the Treasury

Henry Morgenthau landed in New York aboard the *Statendam*, actress Peggy Wood took the *Zaandam*, Dorothy Parker was on the *Veendam*. Those pleasant excursions vanished in the blast of war.

Cor Stapel still remembers the early days of the combat. "Immediately," he says, "the *Nieuw Amsterdam* was converted into a troopship. In the Grand Hall, an extra deck was welded halfway between floor and ceiling. The artistic decorations were stored away until better times. We sailed from San Francisco to New Zealand and Australia. We went to the Middle East, to South Africa, to Scotland. On the tweendeck in the Grand Hall, 500 soldiers sometimes slept.

"We never sailed in convoy. Our jewel of a ship was simply too fast for that. We sailed a zigzag course, and we seldom had to tune up our Chicago piano. The British Navy and reconnaissance aircraft kept a good eye out for U-boats in our vicinity.

"We made journeys of 14, 15 and 16 days without stopping. We had to take risks. Our cooks worked like horses. Two meals a day for 8000 men. A thousand litres of milk a day, 80 sacks of flour, 1100 dozen eggs, 500 kilos of bacon, 6400 litres of coffee and tea, 550 kilos of cold meat, 14,000 slices of bread, 440 kilos of butter. I remember it well because I had to do the purchasing. The tables were always laid.

"It wasn't easy. On our return trips from Europe, carrying the wounded home, the ship stank of pus and blood. There were men lying in bunks with legs and arms shot off. You had to look after them. You had to comfort them.

"It was such a strange time. In Glasgow, we never left the ship. In New York, we had our fun. Sometimes, you came ashore with nine month's pay. You danced. You loved. You drank. Invitations from New Yorkers flew at you. It was the same in Australia. Suddenly, you were a young man, and you were all alone. You didn't hear a word from your family. You cried and you laughed, and you became sentimental, and all the time you kept telling yourself: 'Maybe tomorrow we won't be here any more.'"

HOLLAND-AMER
L

ICA
NE
s.s. Statendam III / 1927

STATENDAM

In the year 1929, production in the United States reached an all-time high, which would not be surpassed until World War II. If you look at early 1929 newspaper reports on the booming economy and photographs of the gaity of the people, it seems difficult to believe that by the end of the year the Wall Street crash would cause the world to shake on its foundations and mark the beginning of a long, almost hopeless period.

It was a year of records. Detroit produced 5,385,000 cars; 24 years — a full generation — later, 5,700,000 new cars were produced. The number of plants and workshops went up from 183,900 in 1925 to 206,700 in 1929, and the value of their total output from 60.8 to 68 billion dollars. The Federal Reserve index for industrial production (based on the years 1923–1925 equalling 100) went from 67 in 1921 to 126 by June, 1929.

Passenger traffic across the Atlantic experienced times of great prosperity in 1929. Tens of thousands of American tourists made the journey to Europe and back. On August 31, for instance, 15 ocean-going steamers sailed from New York: The *Nieuw Amsterdam*, the *Olympic*, the *Berlin*, the *Carmania*, the *Arabic*, the *Albertic*, the *St. Louis*, the *American*

Poster Statendam III, with Dutch fishing vessel. Hull of Statendam III at Harland and Wolff Ltd. shipyards in Belfast.

± 1930

Merchant, the *Hellig Olav*, the *California*, the *Franconia*, the *Conte Biancamano*, the *Minnewaska*, the *Drottingholm*, and the *Provence*. On September 27, the *Rotterdam* sailed in the company of 13 other liners. Society columns in the New York papers printed long lists of prominent passengers.

A clamor accompanied the departure of Thomas W. Lamont, June 28 on the *Statendam*, the beautiful new flagship of the Holland America Line. Lamont of J. P. Morgan & Co. headed a delegation of 150 American bankers and businessmen on their way to attend a meeting of the International Chamber of Commerce in Amsterdam.

His briefcase contained a proposal to boycott trade with countries which did not conform to the Kellogg pact to outlaw wars of aggression as a means to settle desputes. The delegation included C. Bascom Slemp, Howard Coffin, Joseph S. Seligman, John Cregg, Edward A. Filence, Silas H. Strawn and Willis H. Booth, president of the Merchants' Association

of New York. In October of that same year, Thomas W. Lamont and Willis H. Booth were to become two of the men most frequently quoted in their efforts to avert the Depression.

On September 15, the papers contained a story about the wife of the Utrecht professor R. de Josselin de Jong, who, half an hour before the *Veendam* was due to sail on the 14th, discovered that she had left her jewels in her suite of rooms in the New York Pennsylvania Hotel. The no longer young professor De Jong did not hesitate, raced down the gangway and jumped into a taxi on the HAL pier at the foot of 5th Street in Hoboken. Professor De Jong found the jewels — but caused the *Veendam* to depart a half an hour late. From that, the papers concluded that the Holland America Line people weren't just bureaucrats; they had hearts.

On the Atlantic, the major shipping companies tried to outbid one another in speed. The new *Bremen* of the Norddeutscher Lloyd had a speed of 28.5 knots, which made her the world's fastest passenger ship. In New York, Chapman announced the building of two ships of 50,000 tons each. The French wanted to outdo the *Bremen* with a new ship. The Cunard Line had a ship almost completed which would not be fitted with engines until the speed of the French ship was known.

The New York Times wrote sneeringly about the speed race: Did passengers really set so much store by speed? Wouldn't they rather have peace and comfort? Once again the HAL was singled out. Their service even met the exacting standards of the New York Times.

It was a year of hurry and agitation, 1929. A strange year. People believed in miracles about suddenly getting rich. And some people did suddenly get rich. Many others shared in the general prosperity. "Our tourists

travel to Europe with plenty of dollars in their pockets and handbags," a reporter proudly wrote about the thousands of passengers on the ocean-steamers. The Saturday Evening Post published a poem illustrating the belief in quick riches:

Oh, hush thee, my babe, granny's bought some more shares
Daddy's gone out to play with the bulls and the bears,
Mother's buying on tips, and she simply can't lose,
And baby shall have some expensive new shoes!

Prophets of doom were dismissed — or ignored. The last State of the Union message by outgoing President Calvin Coolidge, on December 4, 1928, was still fresh in everybody's memory.

"Never has a Congress of the United States, met to consider the state of affairs in the country, viewed a more gratifying prospect than now is the case. At home there is peace and satisfaction and the highest record of years of prosperity. Abroad peace and good will, the result of mutual understanding, reign." President Coolidge viewed the present with satisfaction and the future with optimism. Contrary to American tradition, he did not attribute this prosperity to the superiority of the government led by him. "The main source of these unequalled blessings lies in the integrity and the character of the American people," he stated.

However, for Captain Cornelis Visser, at that time a ship's mate, the difficult period had already started: "We plied to the Gulf of Mexico, the East and the West coast. I remember that in 1928 there was already very little freight. Things were going badly with the American farmers. In New York, they were too busy to think about it.

General-manager F. W. Rypperda Wierdsma was employed by the Holland America Line to canvas freight in Chicago.

''I had to try and book freight from those enormous slaughterhouses. It took some getting accustomed to. It stank. Before that, I had worked in Geneva and in New York. I started in Geneva in 1926 – don't laugh – getting containerloads of furniture together for Americans who worked at the League of Nations and returned to America. Containers in 1926! There is nothing new under the sun. The shipping of frozen meat and also offal from Chicago to Europe was, for that matter, still big business in 1929.''

J. R. Beck of the HAL in New York had just moved to the new offices at 29 Broadway with the passenger department. ''We had so many plans. The cruises were still doing fine in 1929. Even for a time in '30. For me, the Depression came as a shock. Everything looked so rosy. Everybody was optimistic.''

Adriaan D. Swierstra, who crossed the ocean as an emigrant in 1910 when he was 12, was a HAL accountant at 29 Broadway in 1929. ''The Depression was dreadful, but it really is true that it came as a surprise to us. It was as if the world looked different. All at once you could see former office clerks hawking apples. On West 43rd Street, we counted 19 bootblacks.''

Mate Pieter van Beelen started his career as a seaman in 1929. ''I was allowed to go for one voyage only because I was so insistent. I was single and there was already an instruction that no unmarried mates should be signed on.''

Thomas van Hall was a lodger in 1929 in Rochester, New Jersey. His landlord was a woman who always had a copper pot on the fire. ''I said, 'My, my, you have a big wash every day.' It was not until later that I found out that she was moonshining. Don't forget it was the time of Prohibition! On weekends her friends came from near and far to drink. Some even had their mouths under the tap of the secret boiler to catch the last little drip of alcohol. I have the impression that I just made it in 1929. I was employed as a municipal gardener.''

John Last, in Wayne, New Jersey, remembers writing hundreds of application letters. ''Every day, you scanned the papers for vacancies. One day the telephone rang I had traveled, I knew languages. I could get a job with the Tidewater Oil Company at $ 75 a month, with moderate prospects.''

Labor Day in 1929 was on Monday, September 2. New York was sweltering in a heat wave. Cars returning in the evening after the long weekend caused congestions for miles on the roads leading to town. The next day the late summer sun scorched the city. It was the hottest day of the year. But few people suspected that September 3 would go down in history as the day on which a tragic development began for the Old and the New World.

The New York Herald Tribune announced the marriage of Miss Maude Harrison Perkins, daughter of Mr. and Mrs. Fránk Gordon Perkins of Bloomfield, to Robert Melville Scholle, son of Mrs. Melville Scholle and the late Mr. Melville Scholle of 77 Park Avenue. The couple's honeymoon would be spent on board the *Volendam*, sailing on September 21. In The Hague, the internationally known lawyer Charles Evan Hughes decided to take the *Rotterdam* for the return voyage to New York. He had presided over two sessions of the International Court of Justice and spoke highly of the potential this court had to maintain world peace. On his arrival in New York, he stated that he would support the candidacy of the Republican Fiorella La Guardia for the office of mayor.

And yet, symptoms of a crisis were surfacing. The famous city editor Alexander Dana Noyes of the New York Times was not impressed by the ''miracles'' of the era. He did not believe in fairy tales. Things were not going well in Wall Street. The rapidly rising prices of shares could not go on forever. The chief editor of The Commercial and Financial Chronicle did not mince his words, saying that Wall Street had taken leave of its senses. He kept on warning against the system of buying shares on margin, which was increasingly being viewed as a magic means of getting rich quickly.

The annual report of the Holland America Line for 1928 stated: ''The freight market to America appears to have developed unfavorably. The demand for grain tonnage was small as a result of the high price of grain in the United States and Canada as compared with other countries.''

On the other hand, the management of HAL also wrote: ''The s.s. *Rotterdam* made its usual Mediterranean cruise, the s.s. *Veendam* three successive voyages from New York to the West Indian islands and the s.s. *Nieuw Amsterdam* a voyage from Boston to Havana and back. All these voyages went without hitch to the general satisfaction of the passengers.''

As late as October 3, 1929, C. van de Stadt, general passenger agent for America of the HAL, delivered a cheerful speech on the qualities of the new flagship *Statendam*, and the vitality of his company. He spoke at the Bankers Industrial Exposition in New York. He recalled the way in which the *Statendam* was welcomed by the *Macom*, the ship of New York's mayor. ''It was not only a salute to celebrate the 320th anniversary of the arrival of Hendrik Hudson with *De Halve Maen*, or to the first Dutch colonists on Manhattan who contributed so much to the development of New York City, but also to the Dutch skill in building one of the finest ships for the Europe-America service.'' At the same time, he announced the rebuilding of the *Rotterdam* to make her one of the most modern ships on the Atlantic, at a cost of one million dollars. And he called it a compliment to the *Volendam* that for the second time the ship has been chosen by the New York State Savings Banks to hold an annual meeting during a short cruise to the Caribbean.

September 3, 1929, was a very calm day outside the confines of Wall Street. Years afterwards, Frederick Lewis Allen described it in ''Only Yesterday.'' ''Disarmament is discussed in the usual incoherent way,'' he wrote, ''which will undoubtedly cost us our lives one day.'' A three-engined aircraft of Transcontinental

September 29, 1929. THE SAINT PAUL PIONEER PRESS. SUNDAY, SEPTE...

SCHUBERT CLUB OPENS ACTIVITIES WEDNESDA...

PROMINENT ST. PAUL FOLK IN RECENT ATLANTIC CROSSINGS

European travel continues to attract St. Paulites, many sailing now for a winter abroad, while those who have spent the summer in travel are arriving home. At the left above are Mrs. Charles E. Smith Jr., 596 Grand avenue, and her two daughters, Esther and Mary, who sailed in the past week for a year's stay at the International School in Geneva. At the right above are Mrs. W. A. Dorsey, 459 Portland avenue, and her daughter, Mrs. Philip Elizabeth Dorsey (center). They return from summer travel abroad. Frost and Miss Molly Frost, 544 sailed for three years' study abroad.

—The Statendam, Under the Flag of Holland.

...go to the Seven Seas

NEWARK

Persona...

States."
"Oh, well, let him smoke..."
This smoking on piers is at least ...
President.

Mr. Hughes an...

THE whispered tip has just floated... Mr. Charles Evans Hughes... American liner Rotterdam late la... boat by special tender so he coul... New York ahead of the other gues... have to stay aboard overnight and ... their luggage for the customs ... this morning.

Maybe so, maybe so. But ... Hughes takes advantage of this ... mental courtesy, our guess'll ... again, because he very seldom ... on such favors by officials.

Whenever the jurist come... town there's usually a batch ... seven brass braided and civilia... folks hustling about and stun... each other trying to show him ... And he always stands to ... smiles and tells the boys that ... hurry at all, that it's customa... lans to have their baggage ... he'll wait.

He doesn't exactly detest ... tion; we figure he likes it beca... he hasn't whispered it to us o... fast table lately, it comes u... of amusement to see so many ...

NOW we'll...

October 1, 1929. NEWARK EVENING NEWS.

Personal Activ...

...yn Park Residents Back from Europ...

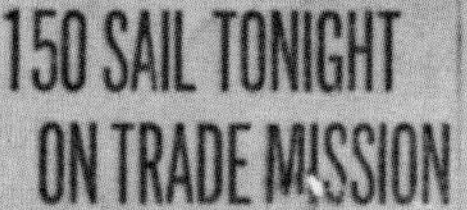

...turning on the New Amsterdam from Europe were Rev. and Mrs. Ralph B. ... of Llewellyn Park. Mr. Pomeroy is clergyman in charge of the Church of th... is a lawyer.

---

150 SAIL TONIGHT ON TRADE MISSION

U. S. Delegation to International C. of C. Hopes to Allay Foreign Fear of Tariff

PLAN RETALIATION OFFSET

Hoping to create in European public opinion an appreciation of the attitude of American business toward tariff, 150 business men are sailing at midnight tonight on the Statendam to attend the Fifth General Congress of the International Chamber of Commerce, which is to be held in Amsterdam, Holland, July 8 to 13. They are the American delegation and are attending the congress under the chairmanship of Thomas W. Lamont.

Trade barriers and tariffs, according to Julius H. Barnes, American vice-president of the International Chamber, will come before the meeting as one of the major subjects of discussion. He declared today that the American delegation is in hearty sympathy with the effort to remove unnecessary obstacles to trade. He explained, however, that, though the United States does not wish to exclude foreign produce, it is necessary to arrange a tariff schedule which will not cause lowering of our wage scales or standards of living.

Must Uphold Living Standard

"We cannot permit in the United States," he said, "destructive competition from abroad which will in any way bring about a lowering of our wage scales and a consequent reduction in American living standards, the highest in the world. It is of far more service to the world to preserve American standards as a goal for other peoples than to permit those standards to be reduced through opening up our markets to an unrestricted current of goods produced by cheaper labor.

"At the same time, we cannot set up here an exclusive policy, because we are depending more and more upon our export trade to keep our plants running. I have been told that one European country is determined to exclude American automobiles, no matter how high a duty it is necessary to impose. That offers an instance of the unwisdom of establishing an exclusion policy here. We do not want to injure a great industry by establishing a policy which may bring retaliations on the part of ...

Soothes Tariff Fears

JULIUS H. BARNES

other countries.

Mr. Barnes said that the point of view which the American delegation plans to bring to Amsterdam is expressed in a statement of American tariff principles which has been sent to the Senate Finance Committee as the opinion of the 1,600 members of the National Chamber. The statement says:

"The American business community declares for maintaining a just protective tariff for American industry and agriculture. Vested with the responsibility of fostering and maintaining America's higher wage scales and living standards, American manufacturers, as also America's agricultural producers, are entitled to just protection against competition in our home markets from world competitors, whose products are those of lower wage scales.

"In the same way, American business declares that it appreciates the benefits of international trade, and that there should be no unnecessary trade barriers.

"American business does not ask exclusion of competition, but does desire a recognition of its sober responsibilities to maintain living standards. These standards must be protected.

"In applying the principle of protection, with the constant changing costs and other factors, business supports the principle of flexible adjustments within the legislative limits fixed by Congress, this flexibility to be maintained and improved in adminis...

...ON TO WASHINGTON—Upon arrival here from Europe aboard S. S. Rotterdam, Charles Evans Hughes, with his wife, immediately left for Washington, where he will preside at water rights hearing...

Mrs. Robert M. Scholle of New York and N... ...sailed last week on the S. S. Volendam for a w... ...ding trip abroad.

...ON TEA AT CIVIC

—Ella Barnett Studio, N. Y.

MR. AND MRS. FRANK PAYNE AND MISS CATHERINE PAYNE

DEAR MARIAN:

ISN'T this an interesting picture of Mr. and Mrs. Payne and their youngest daughter, Catherine Payne? They returned on Saturday on the New Amsterdam, the Holland-American liner, after three ...

ON

Among...
July 13 ...
a summ...

Air Transport crashed during a thunderstorm over Mexico. Eight people were killed. Transcontinental Air Transport had just opened a 48-hour service to the West Coast of America — by railway sleeping-car to Columbus, Ohio, by plane to Waynoka, Oklahoma, by sleeping-car to Clovis, New Mexico, and the rest of the way once again by plane.

The Graf Zeppelin was nearing the end of its first flight around the world. Babe Ruth was leading major league baseball in home runs again. Erich Maria Remarque's "All Quiet on the Western Front" led the best seller list. Fashion continued to accentuate the flat bosom.

The great American writers F. Scott Fitzgerald and Ernest Hemingway, living in Paris far from their hurried country, were central figures of America's "Lost Generation."

On Wall Street, meanwhile, brokers were frantically busy. "The New York Stock

Exchange had a turnover of 4,438,910 shares on September 3," professor John Kenneth Galbraith wrote in "The Great Crash." "The loan-rate all day was at nine per cent. The tariff of banking charges for first-class trade paper was at 6.5 per cent. The bank discount rate of the Federal Reserve Bank in New York was at 6 per cent. The market was firm, with what the stock exchange reporters called a good undertone."

It is generally accepted that September 3, 1929 marked the end of the bull market of the

crash and that crash may be dreadful.' With his usual precision, he stated that the Dow Jones average would most probably fall from 60 to 80 points. He concluded with an avalanche of not very cheerful prospects. 'Factories will close down. Men will be sacked. The vicious circle will begin to exert full force and will result in a serious crisis in economic life.' "

Though America's bubble did not burst until late 1929, other parts of the world were already in serious trouble. While America's top layer was getting rich quickly, there was considerable unemployment in Europe. In Germany, national socialism had begun to

sailed with less than a third of their carrying capacity. Ships were already being laid up, but the worst years were still to come.

Despite the refusal of the Dutch government to give financial support, the building of the *Statendam* was completed at Rotterdam's Wilton shipyard, thanks to the help of a syndicate called "Friends of the Company," founded by Rotterdam citizens For many years the hull had been waiting for completion in a Belfast shipyard, and its eventual completion in Rotterdam was for the HAL the only redeeming feature in a generally gloomy period.

The seeds for the Depression that shook not just the HAL but virtually all international companies were planted during the height of the boom. Share prices on the New York Stock Exchange began to rise by the middle of 1924, company profits were favorable, and by 1927 the boom began in earnest. In that year an act of generous, but ill-founded internationalism began one chain of events that led to the crash of 1929. Later President Hoover would even call it a deed of faithlessness.

The United States had emerged from the First World War as the world's greatest financial power, with New York replacing London as the leading financial center. Britain and France owed America large amounts for the supply of war material, and these countries could only pay off their debt if Germany could discharge the reparation payments imposed by the Treaty of Versailles.

In order to achieve this, America lent money to Germany and invested large sums of money in German enterprises. As a result, Germany was able to carry out reparation payments to France and Britain, which returned the amounts to America to pay for their war debts.

National pride had caused Britain to return to the gold standard in 1925 (under the auspices of the Chancellor of the Exchequer Winston Churchill) at the pre-war rate of exchange between gold, dollars and pounds. Consequently, Britain became an expensive

twenties. Not for more than a decade would the stock exchange show signs of its old self-confidence.

On September 4 the mood was still good, but on the fifth, there was a hitch. The New York Times index fell 10 points, and many stocks lost more than that. The turnover increased sharply, because of the growing pressure to sell. That day 5,565,280 shares changed hands.

"The immediate cause of the fall was evident and interesting," professor Galbraith wrote. "On September 5, Roger Babson, in a speech to the annual national conference for business, said: 'Sooner or later there will be a

spread with Hitler's promise that he would get work for the German laborer. In Italy, fascism with Mussolini was already in power, and in the Netherlands, Britain and other European countries, most people were definitely not flourishing.

The Holland America Line had difficulty keeping its head above water. Freight traffic was doing badly. Due to very poor results, the HAL had withdrawn from the South America Line in 1928. The amount of freight offered by the United States was so small that several ships

±1930

The gay twenties on board
Statendam III.

*1929

country to buy from and an easy market to
sell to.
This began a long series of balance of payments
crises for Great Britain. The poor market for
English coal and the attempt to lower costs
and prices in order to be able to compete
on the world's markets led to the general strike
of 1926 in Britain.

The value of the pound sterling was fixed
at 4.86 dollars. Unreasonably high. The result
was a flight out of pounds to the dollar. And just
as after the Second World War, an enormous
quantity of gold flowed from Europe to Fort
Knox in America. That flow of gold grew so
great that soon many European countries were
forced to drop the gold standard. In view of the
close financial links of the United States with
Britain, France, and Germany, the continuation
of this flow of gold would have meant that the
U.S. would be swept along in a great financial
crisis. Something had to be done.

In the spring of 1927, Andrew W. Mellon,
secretary of the Treasury, and Benjamin Strong,
head of the New York Federal Reserve Bank,
met with three European financial experts, who
came to insist on a policy of cheap money. The
three were Montagué Norman, governor of the
Bank of England; Hjalmar Schacht, governor of
the Deutsche Reichsbank; and Charles Rist,
vice-governor of the Banque de France. The
flow of gold to America could be stopped, they
said, if prices in the United States were high and
the rate of interest low. It would then become
unattractive to buy goods or invest capital.

Their request was granted with some
hesitation over whether the move might
overheat the already active American economy.
The discount rate of the Federal Reserve Bank
of New York was reduced from 4 to 3.5 per
cent. Government bonds were bought. But this
resulted in large amounts of cash becoming
available to the banks and individuals selling
those bonds. With that the fences were down
in America. The cash was invested in stock, or
used to finance the buying of stock on margin

in the expectation that share prices would keep
going up sharply.

The year 1929 has always been the
property of economists so for a long time people
ignored the psychological and social factors
which were also determining factors for the
downfall of the era of foolish hope.

Who knows why thousands of
Americans, after the lowering of the discount
rate, suddenly began to speculate on the stock
exchange with large amounts of call money
borrowed at unprecedented high interest rates?
Why did so many people begin to believe that
they could quickly get rich by simply keeping an
eye on the ticker in the broker's office? What
induced shrewd entrepreneurs to lend their
money for the purpose of buying shares instead
of investing it in their company? Why did
thousands of credulous people hang upon every
word of the great stock exchange figures of
those days, the bull operators John J. Rascob,
William Crapo Durant, the seven Fisher brothers
and Arthur W. Cutten? Why did they send
furious letters to the cautious Alexander Dana
Noyes of the New York Times? Delusion?
Lack of economic wisdom? Too firm belief in
the New Era with its records and technical
ingenuity, its ever bigger ships, airplanes,
zeppelins, radio, movies, lasting peace?
A dance around the golden calf? A desire to
belong in the heady world of diamond rings
and speak-easies? Whatever the reasons, the
outcome was disastrous.

In '28 and '29, money was the most
important thing in the lives of Americans. In
other countries, too, the well-to-do looked
yearningly to the Wall Street paradise. A wide
money flow streamed to New York to enable
speculators to buy shares on margin. Interest of
12 per cent was, after all, 12 per cent, but the
speculators did not mind. Prices kept on rising
so the high interest was quickly earned back.
The money lenders participated in the increased
prices of shares without the burdens and
headaches of share holdings. For them it seemed

a safe way of investing. The loan was backed by
the shares on margin, which could be sold
immediately.

In the brokers' offices, people could be
seen sitting day in, day out, just watching the
blackboard with share prices or the ticker. They
seemed oblivious to their own business. There
were tickers all over the country. Soon they also
made their appearance on ocean steamers, so
that speculators could continue to play their
game even at sea. On August 17, 1929, the
Leviathan and the *Île de France* sailed as the
first ships with branch offices of brokers' firms
on board. On the *Île de France*, Irving Berlin, the
song writer, was one of the first to transact
business. He sold 1,000 Paramount-Famous-
Lasky shares at 71. It was a clever stroke.
Later the price dropped to almost zero as the
company went bankrupt.

On Black Thursday, October 24, 1929, a
dream melted into thin air. That day 12,894,650
shares changed hands at staggeringly low
prices. Wild rumors were going round. Eleven
speculators were said to have already committed
suicide.

At half past eleven, the stock exchange
surrendered to blind fear.

At noon, reporters learned that a meeting
was taking place in the offices of J. P. Morgan
& Co. at 23 Wall Street. Soon the names of the
bankers became known: Thomas W. Lamont,
Albert Wiggin of Chase National, Charles
Mitchell and William Potter of the Guaranty
Trust, Seward Prosser of the Bankers Trust and
George F. Baker Jr. of the First National. The
bankers decided to give the stock exchange
"organized support," which would also be in
their own interest, of course.

At 12:30 the visitors' gallery of the Stock
Exchange was cleared, so that outsiders could
no longer watch the wild scenes. Winston
Churchill was one of those outsiders.

On Tragic Tuesday, October 29, 1929,
the death-blow landed. The organized support
did not work. Rumor was rife... Mitchell had

asked Lamont for a loan for himself… Bankers were shooting themselves with revolvers… In minutes millionaires were reduced to penniless beggars… Later on, things turned out to be not quite so black. It was found that not so many suicides had been committed. Only a few banks had to close down. But the bottom had fallen out of the market. Sixteen million shares changed hands for a song.

⚓ The Holland America Line had to take drastic steps to safeguard its continued existence. The Netherlands was hit by the great depression which immediately followed the Crash of '29. Three hundred thousand unemployed crowded around the dole offices. Unblended margarine, flannel undershirts, tins of spinach and minced meat appeared in government shops.

⚓ Grain transports by the HAL from America fell from 345,000 tons in 1927 to 139,000 tons in 1930 at a freight-rate which "scarcely leaves anything to charge," management told the Supervisory Board. The farmers in Mason City, Iowa, a rich agricultural district, agreed. They only got 10 cents for a bushel of oats and 12 cents for a bushel of corn. They couldn't even pay the freight to ship their produce. All the troubles in the New and the Old World seemed to interlock.

⚓ In the Netherlands, tomatoes went to the compost heap; in Oregon, thousands of apples rotted away, because a case with 200 absolutely perfect apples yielded only 40 to 50 cents. At the same time, children of unemployed workers and of people with sharply reduced salaries could no longer afford to eat apples. In Oregon, shipping a sheep cost $1.10 in 1932 and a sheep sold for only a dollar. Breeders decided to slaughter their flocks.

⚓ In Oklahoma, Texas, Arkansas and Louisiana, hundreds of thousands of bales of cotton rotted on the fields because the pickers could not buy enough beans and meat at the top daily wage of 70 cents to work all day long. And the price of cotton wasn't high enough to justify a better wage. The vicious circle grew increasingly vicious.

⚓ Meanwhile, the HAL was forced to lay up ships; all shipping companies had to. The position of the HAL got so bad that in October 1931, A. F. Bronsing, managing director of the Stoomvaart Maatschappij Nederland, was appointed delegate member of the board of supervisory directors by a meeting of debenture holders. In fact, Mr. Bronsing assumed control of the management of the shipping company.

⚓ The year 1931 brought a loss of 7.7 million guilders for HAL. The only bright spot was the transport of gold, which was now flowing back from America to Europe in small barrels. In 1931, the staff had to be reduced from 3944 with an annual salary of 6.5 million guilders to 2595 with an annual salary of 3.8 million guilders. Officers had to accept a 10 per cent cut in salaries and crew members a 9 per cent cut.

⚓ The HAL offices at the Austrian border, in Budapest, Zagreb and Warsaw, had to close down. The office in Prague was sold. The offices in Berlin and Vienna were merged with the offices of other Dutch companies. In the United States, the Pittsburgh office was closed. In Canada, the office in Winnipeg was discontinued.

⚓ The events at the HAL in the big crisis synchronized with the events in the United States and the Netherlands. Never before had people on both sides of the ocean shared their adversities to such an extent. There were soup lines in Amsterdam and bread lines in New York.

⚓ Songwriter Yip Harburg got famous with his hit, "Brother, Can You Spare a Dime" in the show "Americana."

⚓ "The biggest bread line in New York was run by William Randolph Hearst," Harburg explained in the book "Hard Times" by Studs Terkel.

⚓ "There was a skit in one of the first shows I did, 'Americana.' This was 1930. In the sketch, Mrs. Ogden Reid of the Herald Tribune was very jealous of Hearst's beautiful bread line. It was bigger than her bread line. It was a satiric, volatile show. We needed a song for it.' The prevailing greeting at that time, on every block you passed, by some poor guy coming up, was: 'Can you spare a dime?' Or: 'Can you spare something for a cup of coffee?'"

Menu illustration by Allan Harker.

The New York Tim

VOL. LXXIX....No. 26,206. ★ ★ ★ ★

NEW YORK, THURSDAY, OCTOBER 24, 1929.

PRICES OF STOCKS CRASH IN HEAVY LIQUIDATION, TOTAL DROP OF BILLIONS

PAPER LOSS $4,000,000,000

2,600,000 Shares Sold in the Final Hour in Record Decline.

MANY ACCOUNTS WIPED OUT

But No Brokerage House Is in Difficulties, as Margins Have Been Kept High.

ORGANIZED BACKING ABSENT

Bankers Confer on Steps to Support Market—Highest Break Is 96 Points.

Frightened by the decline in stock prices during the last month and a half, thousands of stockholders dumped their shares on the market yesterday afternoon in such an avalanche of selling as to bring about one of the widest declines in history. Even the best of seasoned, dividend-paying shares were sold regardless of the prices they would bring, and the result was a tremendous smash in which stocks lost from a few points to as much as ninety six.

Loss in Market Values.

The absolute average decline of active and so-called inactive issues yesterday was 2.995, or roughly three points. Using this figure as a base and taking the percentage of shares listed on the Exchange in relation to the percentage of issues traded in, the loss in value of listed securities amounted to $2,210,675,184. This, however, does not measure up to the full value of the loss, for the reason that many lesser-known issues of small capitalization did not

Thyroid Determines if a Man Should Be Flier, Says Dr. Asher

Special to The New York Times.
BALTIMORE, Md., Oct. 23.—Upon perfect thyroid condition depends an airplane pilot's efficiency, declared Dr. Leon Asher, Professor of Physicology at the University of Berne, in an address last evening before the Biological Society School of Medicine of Maryland University.

Persons with a hyper-thyroid secretion have no place in aviation, he continued.

Dr. Asher said he found in experiments that animals with more than the normal thyroid secretion require an excessive amount of oxygen, and are not able to endure a

HOOV'
PLANS
INLAR

In Louis
Proje
to

URGES

Would
share
Lo

ENDS

President Starts for Capital After Being Acclaimed at Madison,

COA
OVE

13 De
Deser
to 37

POWE

Norris
Back
Cope

Spec
WASHINGTON, Oct. 23.—The Democratic-Progressive coalition crumbled in a test of strength with the Republican Old Guard on an important item of the Smoot-Hawley tariff bill in the Senate this afternoon. Thirteen Democrats who almost invariably are members of the coalition, and three Republicans, who are

asserts. Those engaged in the nation-wide commerce," of recruiting and subsidizing—alumni, athletic directors and in some cases college

way development. This would bring the total cost of the projects he outlined to $525,000,000.

"Swords to Plowshares."

This annual increase was equal to the cost of one-half of one battleship.

"If we are so fortunate as to save this annual outlay on naval construc-

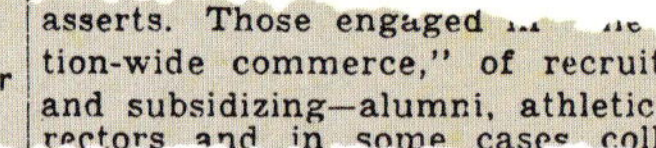
SWIMMING POOL STATENDAM

GYMNASIUM STATENDAM

CUBAN
HAS S

Doumergue Is Not Likely to Find New Premier Soon Because of Party Clashes.

By EDWIN L. JAMES.
Special Cable to THE NEW YORK TIMES.

INSPECTION

Wireless to THE NEW YORK TIMES.
BADEN-BADEN, Oct. 23.—At a

＊1929

CHINESE ROOM STATENDAM

JAPANESE TEA SALOON

The crash of '29 put a stop to the loans from foreigners, who were attracted by the high interest rate for buying on margin. The balance of payments had to be returned to a position of equilibrium after that by a reduction in American exports. And that immediately caused heavy pressure on the export markets for grain, cotton and tobacco, the HAL discovered to its cost.

A chronicle of the great crisis is one litany of misery with only a rare smile. It was not until 1937 that the HAL could breathe a little more freely. Only then could there be thoughts of expanding the staff, of building new ships of opening new offices in the United States and in Europe. Sharp lessons were learned from the long depression. The organization of the shipping company was streamlined.

Economically and socially, the world had not been very well-conceived in the twenties. For one thing, income was badly distributed. Before the crash of '29, the rich were undoubtedly rich. In the United States a top layer of five per cent of the population received about one third of all personal incomes, but a rich man cannot eat more bread than a poor man. Consequently the economy in those years was to a large extent dependent on investments and the buying of luxury goods by that top five per cent. And those purchases and investments were badly affected by the crash of '29.

There was a lot of economic clumsiness in the twenties era which led to trouble: poor industrial set-up, bad organization of banking, a doubtful balance of payments situation, and perhaps above all, a lack of economic insight. The spirit of that time prevented the kind of initiatives that were needed to allay the crisis immediately after the crash. Most statesmen were in favor of letting matters run their course. Everybody suffered under a feeling of infinite hopelessness. It seemed that simply nothing could be done about the great crisis.

Unemployment figures in the United States went up, almost without cease, between

HAL expansion in New York:
from Hoboken to Pier 40.
Arrival passengers,
Holland America Cruises,
Pier 40.
1874-1970

March, 1930, and March, 1933, from 3,250,000 to 14,300,000. Even in the winter of 1937–1938 there were still well over 11,000,000 unemployed. The wages in industry dropped from $28.50 per week in '29 to $22.64 in '31. A startling number of people broke adrift in order to earn at least something by taking odd jobs in various parts of the country. Wandering youngsters went from town to town, from food distribution center to food distribution center, hitchhiking on the long distance trains. Whole families journeyed in their Model-T Fords on worn tires to other areas, hoping for the best.

At a smaller, but no less bitter scale, the same could be seen in the Netherlands. Men went to unemployment relief work. Unemployment benefits dropped to 13 guilders per week. People were starving. Others were tormented by the thought that they would soon be starving.

A few bitter yet amusing facts from those years: Before the crash of '29 nobody ever wanted to serve on a jury in the United States. After the crash, people were jostling in the hall of the Criminal Courts Building of New York; a juror was paid four dollars a day. More than 100,000 Americans reacted to an advertisement of Amtorg in New York for 6,000 skilled laborers for industry in the Soviet Union. One morning in October, 280 passed through the recruitment agency. They included two hairdressers, one funeral director, two plumbers, five painters, two cooks, thirty-six office clerks, nine carpenters, one pilot, fifty-eight engine drivers, fourteen electricians, five salesmen, two printers, two chemists, one shoemaker, one librarian, two teachers, one cleaner, eleven car mechanics and one dentist.

It did not take long after the crash before Hoovervilles of crates and corrugated sheets sprang up in the parks of the big cities, built by people who had been forced to leave their homes, because they could no longer pay their rent. The one in New York in Central Park, near the Obelisk, was called "Hoover Valley." The shadow town was even officially registered under this name with the authorities. One man called his structure "Radio City." He was the only one with a radio set. All neighbors were allowed to come and listen to the uninterrupted stream of bad news. Another christened his abode "Rockside Inn." Yet another thought of "Custer's Last Stand." A street with 17 of these hovels had the nameplate "Depression Street."

STATENDAM

s.s. Statendam IV/design Rein Dirksen/1956/poster detail

1972
Docklift.
Lash-ship Bilderdyk.
Gravel suction-dredger
Deepstone.
Female apprentice officer.
Cut-away drawing of
container-ship Atlantic Star.

Everything today is aimed at using the air. Stand at a bar in New York that has an Irish name and then stand at a bar in a 747 plane, stand without even swaying, and in only a few hours you are in Shannon, at a real Irish bar.

Man has walked, driven and laughed on the moon. Our main source of information and entertainment is television. Live television, direct from the moon to your living room. Direct from Saigon to Rotterdam. From London to Bombay. News from Saigon. A song from Rome. All through the air.

But always there is the sea. The sea's waters cover 70.8 per cent of the earth. And the Dutch poet and biologist Dick Hillenius reminds us, "Once man crawled from the sea onto land. Once man will return to the sea."

And in October of 1972, in a shipbuilding yard in Japan, the largest ship in the world began to slide down the ways. Scaffolding snapping, workers yelling, the *Globtik Tokyo*, 447,000 tons, 379 meters long, twenty-five stories high, slid into the water with a huge splash. Man returns to the sea.

In this same month, along the Wilhelminakade in Rotterdam, the *Docklift 1*, two mobile portal cranes on its deck reaching high into the sky, was handed over the "Big Lift," a new Holland America Line subsidiary. The *Docklift 1* is a self-propelled drydock. It can carry such as nuclear reactor vessels, cracking towers, parts of drilling rigs, dredgers and push barges. The mobile portal cranes are capable of lifting 320 tons each. In the era of man using air, there appears on the waters of the Atlantic the first vessel in history capable of transporting complete dredgers. Man returns to the sea.

And at sea, of a dark night on the Atlantic, an escalator carries you from the main deck of the container ship *Atlantic Crown* to the engine room. Engineers sit in a soundproofed neonlit space. They monitor panels of dials and red and green lights which flash on and off. A datalog punches onto paper tape letters and figures. At high speed the tape gives computations on fuel, temperature, speed, propellor revs, draught, amount of drinking water aboard, and the condition of the cargo. The facts and figures about the cargo are transmitted at the same time over a communications network of the Datel 600. The cargo information goes to Europe and then to the United States. To all customers and clients and brokers and others interested in the cargo being carried through the water.

One hundred years after the founding of the Holland America Line, the shipping business seems to be coming out of the lethargy which aviation created.

Once there was resignation. A captain looking up from his bridge to see the smoke plumes of a 600-mile an hour jetliner high in the sky over the ocean. High in the sky over his slumping, plodding ship. Today, there is daring enterprise instead of resignation. There are

Cargo. Now and then. Replica of The Half Moon, the ship of Hendrik Hudson, founder of New Amsterdam.

±1920

±1972

new shipping businessmen who see land, air and sea routes as one.

The planes which once drove the passenger liners from the waters of the world now fly the passengers to ships which prowl about the most beautiful places on earth. Passenger ships now are being launched as floating hotels not methods of transportation. In shipping lines offices, these new business-men of the oceans plan for the decades ahead.

Sixty per cent of the world's oil is now carried by ship. In the United States, the state of Delaware has published a plan to build an artificial super harbor, some eight miles off the Delaware coast, to handle the great tankers. The British shipping company Globtik Tankers Limited, with its new 447,000 ton ship built in Japan, is only starting. Before 1980, the first million ton vessels with a draught of 35 meters will be on the seas.

And everywhere, work is in progress to extend old harbors and build new ones.
Which is where *Docklift 1* comes in. The transport of dredging plants and parts of oil rigs for the exploration of new sources of energy at the bottom of the sea renders the design and construction of such a unique vessel as a must.

The main concept of an organization such as the Big Lift subsidiary of Holland America Line in the transport from door to door and from factory to building site. All forms of transportation figure in this concept. The shipping segment of the journey is now directed to the transportation of heavy material and bulk cargo such as oil, ore, grain, chemicals, paper and iron.
It is left to the airlines to carry instruments and delicacies like choice fruit. The fleet of passenger ships aims at the leisurely traveler without a specific destination. Being at sea has become a recreation rather than a trip.

One wonders, at this point one hundred years after the bridge across the sea from Rotterdam to New York, what steelman Henry Bessemer would think.
In 1875 his solution for seasickness, the steamship *Bessemer,* with its suspended salon, was made useless by the introduction of another remedy, the catamaran, with its two hulls. And then it all became ludicrous when a chemist strolled out of a laboratory with the ingredients for a simple pill which went so far to cure the malady.

What a science-fiction invention such a sea giant as the *Globtik Tokyo* would have seemed back in 1919 to the New York writer W. J. Abbot. *(The Story of our Merchant Marine.)* But his wonder was directed to the past, at such ships as the first steamship to bridge the Atlantic between Boston and England, the *Savannah*. She was 320 tons in ballast with a 90 hp steam engine to drive two ten-bladed paddles!

Could the British shipbuilder Symington, whose *Charlotte Dundas* was the first tugboat,

Cruises today: The ship, a floating hotel. A base for discovery. Relaxation. The aircraft, link between home and harbor. Tourism, a gigantic industry. The world has been opened up. (Cuts from pamphlets.)

have suspected, in 1802, that one day vessels would appear on the Atlantic transporting complete dredgers?

One hundred years after the bridge over the Atlantic. Jules Verne's boldest fantasies have become reality. The world has been opened up. The world has become accessible.

A man from Frankfurt, West Germany, locks the door of his third floor apartment. Three weeks later he tells his friends that he visited the Borobudur in Java, Indonesia, talked with Moslems, Hindus, and Buddhists, and is deeply impressed by the new buildings he saw in Singapore and Djakarta.

A young woman from New York says goodbye to her family at Kennedy Airport. Two weeks later she is home, projecting 35 mm slides of a cruise she took from Mombasa to Zanzibar. Still under the spell, she sniffs the scent of fresh cloves and hangs an African mask on the wall.

A man from Helsinki shuts his fur shop. Three weeks later he's telling his clients that in Caracas you can buy four different sorts of fruit punch on the street. Dreamily he remembers the evenings in South America, hearing the mysterious sounds of the music from the Andes Mountains.

A student from Montreal shuts his school books. Two weeks later he's back telling his friends that the last Stone Age people in the Baliem Valley of New Guinea are excellent agriculturalists.

An architect puts the light out above his drawing board in Berlin. Two weeks later he brings back a well-documented report on the possibilities of building a new city in India.

A street vendor from the Albert Cuyp open-air market in Amsterdam stores his stand in the warehouse. Two weeks later he's back telling his customers that in Hong Kong hundreds of people really do live on what to his eyes are "strange boats."

The hard-working, well-tanned geologist from Houston goes to sea from time to time because he feels restless on land. He comes back telling fascinating stories about looking for gold and silver in desolate areas of South America, or in parts of Africa.

In the 1970s people are on the move. Like never before. Exploring all parts of their own country, their neighbor's, their entire continent, and others. Europeans, for example, are now voyaging easily to such exotic spots as an Indian Ocean island, there perhaps to spend several hours roaming through a deserted old cemetery. How curious to read the tombstone inscriptions and to realize that not so very long ago inhabitants of such places died young, from the harshness of the very climate which is now one of its tourist attractions.

How long ago is it, in fact, that people trained and prepared for months, and then took huge medical kits, on trips down the Nile, across deserts, to the slopes of the Wilhelmina peaks in New Guinea? Or how long ago is it that a whole family would turn out to wish ''good trip'' when one of its members was going only so far as across a not very distant border?

Forty, thirty, twenty years? The spectacular developments in travel tourism in the last ten years — in the ability of practically anyone to travel practically anywhere — can be called no less than revolutionary.

Witness the changes in sea travel, now considered recreational. ''To me sailing is like a life one has never lived, but a life whose existence one has always suspected,'' comments the old emigrant Thomas van Hall on the quiet Caribbean beach of the Isla de Margarita. Could the United States citizen John Last ever have dreamed — when he started work as a young immigrant at the Tide Water Oil Company at 75 dollars a month in the twenties — that one day he and his wife would make yearly Caribbean

"Sea" Cruise
Week End
in Bermuda
ERICA LINE
RATES AND ITINERARIES
Spotless Fleet
CRUISES
TO WEST INDIES & SOUTH AMERICA
WINTER - SPRING
1938 ● 1939
NEW HOLLAND AMERICA LINER
"STATENDAM"
NIEUW AMSTERDAM - STATENDAM
ROTTERDAM - VOLENDAM
5 to 46 DAYS
CUBA   TRINIDAD   VENEZUELA
PUERTO RICO JAMAICA   BRAZIL
VIRGIN ISLANDS THE BAHAMAS PERU
PANAMA CANAL   CHILE
CURACAO   ARGENTINA
MARTINIQUE   URUGUAY
BARBADOS   BERMUDA
HOLLAND
HOLLAND
AMERICA
LINE
DESCRIPTION
CLASS CABIN
RYNDAM"
Mediterranean and
Norway
CRUISE SENSATION
South America
West Indies
ONLY $
120 UP
BY THE MAGNIFICENT
S.S. STATENDAM.
'77
of the
olendam
South America
and the West Indies
$19
TOURS · HOLLAND-AMERI
THE MODERN SECOND CLASS
HOLLAND-AMERICA LINE
NEW YORK · ROTTERDAM   ROTTERDAM · NEW YORK

Holland America
Around the World
Cruise 1972

on the Friend Ship Rotterdam
87 days – 19 ports
from New York City, January 19, 1
from Port Everglades, January 21,

Holland America
Spring 1971
Grand Orient Cruise

SS Statendam – 52 days
from San Francisco, March 21, 1971
from Los Angeles, March 22, 1971

Holland America
North Cape Cruises
Featuring Leningrad

nd Ship, SS Statendam,
k June 3 and July 16, 1971

Holland America
The Newly-Rebuilt
Friend Ship Statendam
Spring Mediterranean

Holland America Around the World Cruise
on the Friend Ship Rotterdam – Jan. 1973
89 days – 24 ports

From New York Jan. 18, 1973
From Port Everglades, Jan. 20, 1973

Holland America
9 and 11-day
cruises to
the West Indies
April through
December 1970.

Holland America's
Never Before
7-Day Nassau Cru
s.s. Rotterdam

every Saturday, from New Yor
starting April 1973

Holland America

West Indies
Cruises

eptember
to
ay 1970/1971

America's

eldomvattend
se programma 1973

Holland America
The Newly-Rebuilt
Friend Ship Statendam
North Cape C
Featuring Le

From New York – June 9

Holland
America
Cruises

Holland America

Friend Ship
Nieuw Amsterdam

West Indies
Cruises

from Port Everglades, Florida
Nov. 1971 through May 1972

Holland America

Friend Ship Rotterdam

9-Day
West Indies
Cruises

from New York
April through December, 1972

Guide

rella Ship
dam

d America

wly-Rebuilt
Ship Statendam

nd
ribbea

America

wly-Rebuil
tendam an
terdam

st Ind
ises

New York
er 1972 – Apr

The
Supercruisetour
to Europe '72

Holland America
North Cape
Cruise Mercury

Holland America
Cruise Catalogue
1971/1972

A handy listing of hundreds of
luxury cruises to and from ports
all over the world. Ranging from
3-day cruises in the Aegean, to an
87-day cruise around the world

Holland America
s.s. Nieuw Amsterdam
West Indies
Cruises

glades, Florida
gh Dec. 1973

Holland America Cruises
& Partners

Programma 1972

Holland Ame
Around the W
Cruises

The SS Rotterdam is of Netherlands Registry

± 197

Modern advertising.
Round the world.
Fourteen days Singapore-Bali.
Combination flying-cruising.

cruises solely for pleasure? Such a dream has become the reality for millions of people in this hurried society of ours.

The HAL, situated as "The Line" in the heart of Rotterdam, world's largest port, and as Holland America Line and Holland America Cruises on the new pier 40 in New York, at one time was in a masculine business. Now the first young ladies make their appearance on the bridge of ships as qualified "steerswomen."

That future is downright fascinating. In the short term there are for a country like the Netherlands the protectionist measures of budding maritime nations. These make it difficult for the Netherlands, which always proclaimed free trade on a free sea, to maintain its possition.

Once this was done by sea battles in the seventeenth century. Now, only by appealing to reason does this country on the North Sea try to maintain its share in world shipping.

In the long term, however, possibilities arise which go beyond the imagination. In the long term vessels loom on the horizon which seem to come straight from the fantasies of science-fiction writers.

We only begin the exploration of the bottom of the sea, the continental shelf, slopes, volcanic mountain ranges many thousands of meters below sea level.

We first discover them.

Using the sea for other purposes than sailing and fishing is still in its infancy. W. Langeraar, a Dutch scientist of international repute, writes. "However paradoxically it may sound, large tracts of the surface of the moon are better known at the moment than the submerged part of the earth's surface. In fact it was not until during and after the Second World War that an interest was shown for scientific exploration of the sea. Oceanography was not acknowledged and accepted as important until the beginning of the International Geophysical Year in 1957."

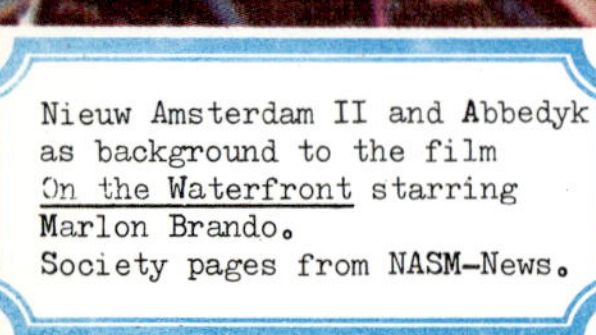
Nieuw Amsterdam II and Abbedyk
as background to the film
On the Waterfront starring
Marlon Brando.
Society pages from NASM-News.

...NA HORNE, singer of popular songs, (with her pug Nellie), ... entertainment luminaries and ...cent Nieuw Amsterdam passengers.

...torian PROF. ARNOLD TOYNBEE ... breezes during a Nieuw Amsterdam

YEHUDI MENUHIN, celebrated concert violinist, also was a flags... traveler, with Mrs. Menuhin, Gerard, 6, and Jeremy, 2½.

FILM FOLK who enlivened reception at first port of call were Cary Grant (left), who was a passenger from Antwerp and Miss Betsy Drake, his leading lady, who greeted him (center) and Captain Theunis Stuut, master of the ship.

Actrice Debbie Reynolds en acteur James Garne... filmopnamen door nog wel even tijd om zich ... van de Statendam op de gevoelige plaat te ...

Dr. J. Robert Oppenheimer, Chief Atomic Energy Commission Adviser.

PIERRE MONTEUX, noted former conducto... of the San Francisco Symphony, a N.A.S.M. regular, arrived at Montreal on the Ryndam.

Movie star George Raft arrived on Nieuw Amsterdam from location on picture in Africa.

Stage, screen and radio are always well represented aboard the Nieuw Amsterdam. Stars studding recent passenger lists included FREDERIC MARCH and FLORENCE ELDRIDGE (left); the famed ANDREWS SISTERS, Maxene, Patty and Laverne (left to right), who gave with some pre-sailing harmonies; screen actress LINDA CHRISTIAN and canine travelmate, shown in an arrival reunion with husband TYRONE POWER.

Al Hirschfeld, premier caricaturist, off to London on assignment to make special curtain for "Drop of a Hat."

DR. GEORGE GALLUP polls MRS. GALLUP who registers approval of Nieuw Amsterdam service.

Mr. Dave Brubeck and his family chose first class accommodations on the November 9 sailing of the s.s. Rotterdam for a "relaxing" trip to Europe where the renowned jazz musician planned a series of concerts.

AL CAPP of "Li'l Abner" fame, daughter Mrs. Michael Pierce (standing), Mrs. Capp, son Colin, nephew Todd Capp and Michael Pierce sailed on the Nieuw Amsterdam.

Nieuw Amsterdam travelers: Clark Gable, Mrs. Gable and her children Adolph and Joan Spreckels (10 and 8½).

UNLIKE THE C...

PROBLEM of transporting his family of nin... to Joannes Griffioen of Utrecht—he chose the... April 24 all spic and span, smiling and co... Hoboken waterfront was the prime event of th... The family, which was headed for a farm...

...horous French film star ...NIELLE DARRIEUX ...gly "framed" herself for ...A.S.M. News cameraman.

Movie star Van Heflin, with Mrs. Heflin and son Tracy, with Commodore Coenraad Bouman on Nieuw Amsterdam's bridge.

Passengers Aboard Were . . ."

Virginia Mayo

...burn, film actress, made a round ...ce on Holland-America flagship.

...whirling dervish of the jazz ...with his new bride, the former ...ler. Krupa took famed quartet ...n European tour.

A BOB HOPE FAN HAS REAL STARS IN HER EYES

YOUNGSTERS in the Nieuw Amsterdam's passenger list mobbed comedian Bob Hope for autographs during his recent crossing in Holland-America Line's flagship. Here he is shown in a typical group. Little girl at upper right has real stars in the pupils of her eyes—a phenomenon caused by refraction from photographer's flashlight reflector. One little boy (who shall be nameless) pushed his way curiously to foreground. Upon discovering cause of excitement he walked away disgruntled. "Aw, thought it was a puppet show," he said.

Henriette Davids, Dutch character actress, as she sailed on the Nieuw Amsterdam.

French Movie Star and Hollywood's Typical Prussian DENISE VERNAC AND ERICH VON STROHEIM

Na een tournee door de Verenigde Staten keerde de Nederlandse jazz-pianiste Pia Beck met de „NIEUW AMSTERDAM" naar huis terug. Tot ieders genoegen werd zij bereid gevonden een concert voor de passagiers te geven. En pas nadat ook de bemanning haar had kunnen horen, kon zij werkelijk van een welverdiende rust genieten.

Armando Serodio, Lisbon

HIS MAJESTY King Leopold III of the Belgians (right), with his wife, Princess de Rethy and Prince Baudouin as they sailed from Lisbon in January for a vacation to Cuba and U. S

DR. HERMAN B. BARUCH
Greeted by Famous Brother, Bernard M.

FILM STAR DEBORAH KERR AND DAUGHTER ON THE NIEUW AMSTERDAM

Captain J. A. J. Reedyk is introduced to Princess Beatrix by Mr. P. C. van Houten, Managing Director of the Holland-America Line from Rotterdam.

De Nederlandse auteur Jan de Hartog, enige tijd geleden in het nieuws na het verschijnen van zijn ophef makend boek "The Hospital", maakte de vorige maand samen met zijn echtgenote een ontspannende zeereis met de Prinses Margriet van Rotterdam naar New York.

FAMOUS AUTHOR—Thornton Wilder, renowned author and playwright, sailed from New York last February on the Ryndam. His destination was Frankfurt, Germany, where he attended the premier of the opera "Alcestiade," for which he wrote the libretto.

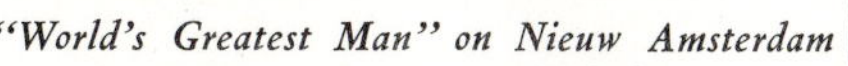

"World's Greatest Man" on Nieuw Amsterdam

In gezelschap van zijn echtgenote stapte de in Nederland zeer gevierde kleinkunstenaar Toon Hermans aan boord van de Nieuw Amsterdam, die hem naar New York bracht, waar hij voorbesidingen ging treffen voor zijn optreden op Broadway volgend jaar. Nadat hij zich vlak voor vertrek van Rotterdam welwillend had laten belegeren door een vijftigtal tv-, radio- en krantenverslaggevers gaf hij de aanwezige persfotografen even spontaan de gelegenheid een leuk plaatje te maken. Waar kan dat beter dan op de brug? Zoontje Gaby, die zijn vader en moeder wegbracht, was echt wel wat bedrust plotseling achter het „stuur" van zo'n groot zeeschip te staan.

News Events

DR. ALBERT SCHWEITZER AND COMMODORE C. H. P. COSTER

Begeleid door de gezagvoerder, Kapitein A. de Jong, betreden Maarschalk Tito en zijn echtgenote de „ROTTERDAM".

De wereldberoemde dirigent Leopold Stokowski komt per Nieuw Amsterdam in Rotterdam aan.

N WHO LIVED IN A SHOE — MR. GRIFFIOEN KNEW WHAT TO DO

Atlantic presented no difficulty ...am, on which they arrived on ...bed. Their descent upon the ...pictures made front page news. ...ia, reads, from left to right: Joseph, in lifering, (1); Franciscus, (2); Elisabeth, (3); Arnoldus, (5); Marianne, (6); Alexandrina, (8); Anna, (10); Maria, (11); Johannes W., (13); Gysberta, (15); Lucas, (17); Joannes, Jr., (18); Lucie, (19); Catharina, (22); Cornelia, (21); Henriette, (21); and Joanna, (22), and last but not least the proud parents. In addition, the party included one adopted son, Piet Mauriks, (18) and one son-in-law, Gysbert van den Brink, (22), married to Catharina.

Nel van Vliet of Holland, world champion swimmer, as she arrived on the Westerdam.

FILM STAR Paulette Goddard and best seller author Erich Maria Remarque were numbered among the 2,078 who departed on company ships during the week ending July 3. They sailed June 27 on Nieuw Amsterdam where they are shown, with Commodore Pieter H. G. Verhoog, on a crossing earlier in the year.

Today, aquanauts go to the bottom of the sea for a stay of several weeks. Self-propelled drilling platforms of the American "Global Marine Inc." cruise on all the world seas. Thousands of meters below samples are drawn from the bottom of the sea. Television cameras observe mysterious rectangles on places at the bottom of the Atlantic where man still cannot venture. We have so far to go.

Drilling platforms on the continental shelf in the North Sea and in the Gulf of Mexico are the forerunner of a fantastic range of instruments which will open up the bottom of seas and oceans. And, hopefully, open the riches of sea water to feed the population of the world, and meet the growing demand for chemical substances and minerals. Submarines with sucking action and tracking equipment crawl across the ocean bottom having passed beyond the stage of imagination. He who can get sand from the depth of the sea can also get other things out of it. Gravel, gold, diamonds, tin, iron, lead. The sea contains all known minerals and chemicals.

Engineers of "Deepsea Ventures Inc." in Virginia are looking for a method to bring to the surface precious manganese, which is for the taking at a depth of 4,000 to 5,000 meters. To win manganese, "Deepsea Ventures" has already carried out a non-commercial experiment at a depth of 1,000 meters on the Blake Plateau off the coast of America. "Deepsea Ventures Inc." hopes to make a start with the commercial mining of billions of tons of metals in 1975. Work will then be carried out at a depth of 4,000 to 5,000 meters. The ships which will collect the lumps operate like a super vacuum cleaner.

Divers in pressure chambers can already carry out their work at a depth of six hundred meters on the slopes of the continental shelf. The Dutch hydraulic engineer J. de Koning has succeeded in quarrying layers of sand to a depth of seventy meters by means of a self propelled suction-dredger.

Before 1970 no one went down with a suction-dredger to any depth beyond thirty meters. De Koning puzzled a great deal, made calculations, arrived at a mathematical formula, and simply fitted the pump under water required for the sucking. He took the pump to the source. This made it possible to penetrate with force through the strata of mud in order to get at the sand underneath and bring it up.

This is only the beginning. The beginning of another revolution. Now seventy meters, tomorrow 80, 140, 240, thousands? Heavier pumps? Giant suction-dredgers? To bring up sand from the silent depths of the sea is to bring up many other things as well …

Where is the link between shipping and oceanography? Lumps of manganese must be brought ashore. Natural gas and oil recovered at sea require tankers. Big Lift's *Docklift 1* is but a foretaste of the strange vessels which will be required in future to supply factories working at sea, and to transport equipment and tools.

One hundred years after the bridge across the Atlantic was built, we look with nostalgia at a poster of a mother and small daughter in Dutch costumes and a three masted ship and a plume of coal smoke trailing from a funnel. "Where is that ship going?" the small girl asks. "To America, my child," the mother says.

At the time, the mere words on the poster, "To America" inspired awe in Rotterdam. In this time we look up, as a Boeing 747 roars through the sky, carrying over 300 passengers on a trip jetting forward at 900 kilometers per hour, at heights of ten to eleven kilometers above. Yet what small matter really is a period of only one hundred years in history?

More than one hundred years ago, the large packet boats from Hamburg, Rotterdam,

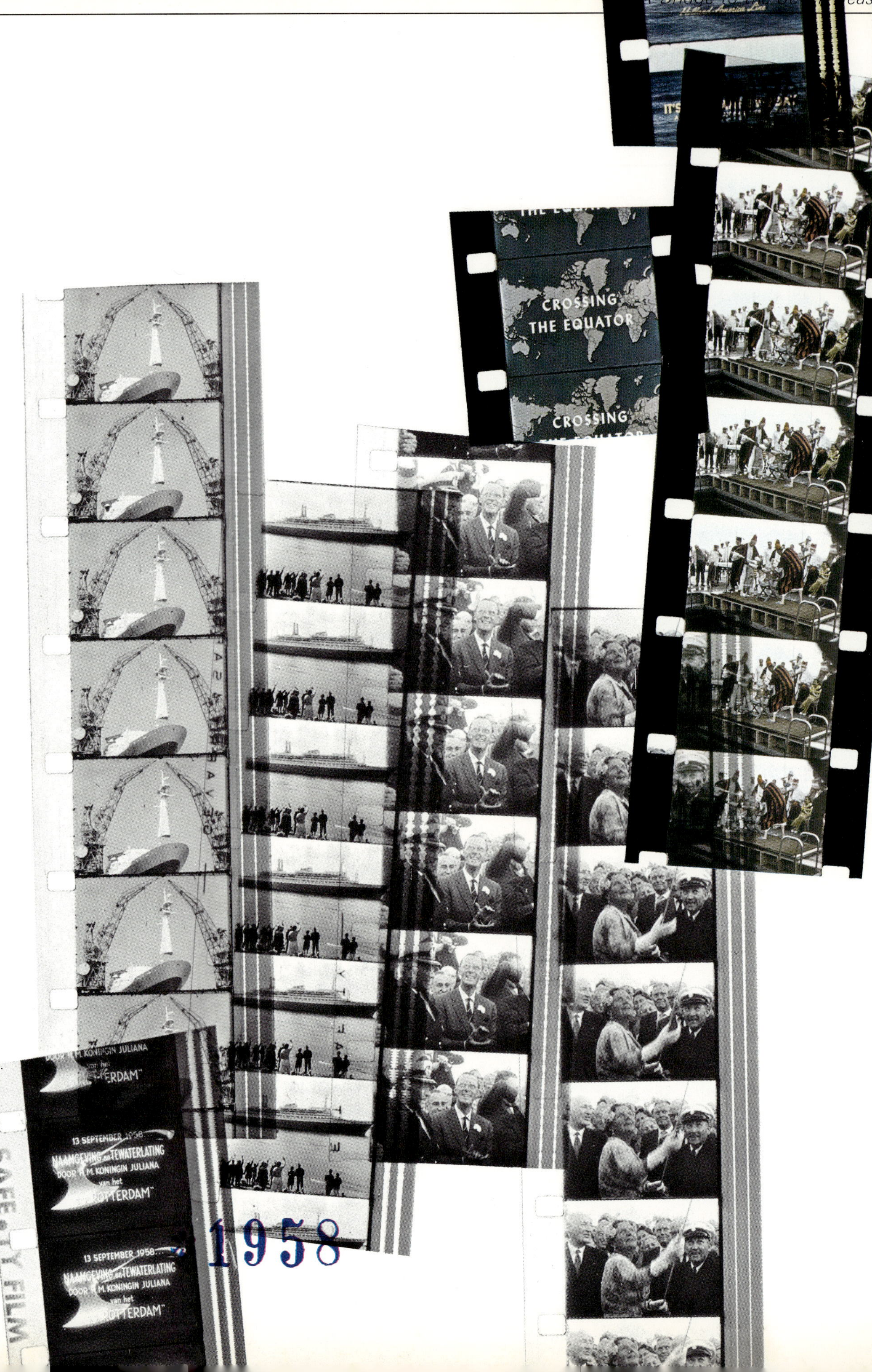

From HAL film archives:
Maiden trip Nw. Amsterdam II.
World cruises. Queen Juliana
and Prince Bernhard on board
Rotterdam V.

Le Havre made their way to America and they depended upon what the Holland America Line did at the time. Mail. The mail contract meant people waited 8 to 10 days for a letter to cross the ocean. Today the New York Times reaches Amsterdam the same day that it is printed in New York City.

And in this one hundred years of ships sailing the seas from Rotterdam to New York, there have been ships carrying whiskey into America at the time of Prohibition, and then there were the quite sizable shipments of gold from America to Europe, as a result of the cheap money policy of the United States at the time of the shipments. It came at the onset of the thirties, a time of gloom in the shipping industry.

On the American side, barrels of gold were transported to the pier in armored trucks and placed on board under heavy guard. Twenty-three million dollars worth of gold was placed on the *Nieuw Amsterdam,* sailing from New York to Boulogne. This was on a crisp fall morning in October of 1931.

The ship left and crossed the ocean uneventfully. The gold was taken off at Boulogne by the tender *Holland*. The Holland America Line representative had asked the French authorities for extraordinary precautions to protect this great shipment.

The unloading operation took from two until five in the morning. The weather was cold and blustery.

The Holland America Line representative stood with his hands turning raw while he watched the cargo being unloaded. He was elated when he was given a receipt for the shipment by a Paris bank official. However, he was surprised to find no railway wagon waiting to carry the shipment to Paris.

The barrels of gold were loaded onto two lorries and covered with tarpaulin. They looked like herring barrels.

The representative from the bank in Paris appeared. He was to supervise the rest of the journey.

The Holland America Line man said, "Haven't

Romantic memory of the tender Holland on the roads off Boulogne-sur-Mer.

R. Wyngaerd
Boulogne sur Mer
21. Rue Victor Hugo.
…r in Boulogne sur Mer, France where
…sengers from Paris. It is on this tender
…m in 1895, with her father, who landed on the ship.
…leave with her. The trip across took 17 days.
…ss. Many times, returning from USA, did my French grandmother
…pick me up here, and I'd stay with her. J.A.R.

N. A. S. M. NEWS

Netherlands' Royal Family Plays Prominent Part in Ship's Early Career

H. M. QUEEN JULIANA is welcomed aboard new pride of Dutch merchant marine by Commodore Bouman at Rotterdam on August 19 for taking-over ceremony. She is accompanied by Mr. de Monchy, H. R. H. Prince Bernhard and Joint President-Director William N. H.

van der Vorm. That day, in the North Sea, Her Majesty hauls N. A. S. M. flag to radar-mast when vessel became the official flagship of the Holland-America Line fleet, proudly assisted by Boatsman Hendrik A. Kluver and Quartermaster Adrianus B. van Lieburg.

Following commissioning rites, Her Majesty held al fresco investiture on sports deck when she decorated Cornelis J. Engelen and Gerardus van Veen (back to camera) of company's new building department with Knight's degree in the Order of Orange Nassau. At the same time the Queen awarded the Knight's degree in the Order of the Netherlands Lion to

Kornelis van der Pols, managing director of the Rotterdam Drydock Co., builders of the ship. At right, Her Majesty inspects Ritz Carlton room. Mr. de Monchy expounds on decorations. Princess Margriet is just entering doorway and Chief Steward Johan W. van Hillen stands just inside. Queen was amazed at transfiguration of ship in twelve months.

N. Y. WELCOMES ROTTERDAM

Continued from Page Two

the supervisor of the town of Rotterdam, New York. The American Rotterdam is a suburb of Schenectady which, with 28,000 inhabitants, is about one-thirtieth the size of the original Netherlands city. The New York State town was settled by Dutch pioneers over three hundred years ago and is very proud of its Dutch antecedents.

Mr. Kirvin brought the official greetings of little Rotterdam to big Rotterdam to be carried back to Burgomaster Gerard E. van Walsum. A duplicate of the framed message was handed to Commodore Bouman for the ship. Both Rotterdams have the same official seal, which the Netherlands Government authorized Rotterdam, N. Y. to adopt.

As these ceremonies were taking place, the scene around the Rotterdam, with the constant buzzing of the photographers' planes, helicopters and other light aircraft, was like a swarming of bees. A flotilla of tugs and small harbor vessels, passing liners and freighters, added to the din with their toots and whistles, while the Fire Department provided an accompaniment of curtains of cascading water.

Passing Tompkinsville, S. I., Commodore Bouman dipped the Dutch flag at the gaff, the same red, white and blue emblem that Henry Hudson carried on the Half Moon. He was paying tribute to that other great skipper whose intrepidity loosed a vast tide of commerce that now pours in and out of what has since become the world's greatest port.

The Rotterdam sailed back on the second half of her maiden voyage to the Channel ports and Rotterdam on September 22. She had a full load of passengers, and a tired but happy and proud crew whose splendid cheerfulness

Continued on Page Four

Her Majesty Queen Juliana and Joint President-Director Willem H. de Monchy at dinner celebrating Rotterdam's addition to fleet which 700 distinguished guests attended.

PRINCE BERNHARD and Princess Irene (center), went aboard Rotterdam just before vessel sailed on maiden voyage from Rotterdam on September 3 to wish Princess Beatrix bon voyage. In center photograph the Princess enjoys a game of shuffleboard in mid-Atlantic with Foreign Minister Luns. At right she gets nautical instruction from Commodore Bouman.

*1959

you got anybody to guard this load ? Do you just leave it up to lorry drivers ?''
The French bank representative beamed. He patted his pocket. ''Mais oui, j'ai un revolver.'' The frozen shipping man went back to his cabin. The French man took a deep gulp of the cold morning air, again patted his pistol, and slipped into the second lorry. The lorries took off for Paris.

Today, the sail-steamship can be admired only in maritime museums, paintings and models. One hundred years after the departure of the very first *Rotterdam* to New York on 15 October 1872 with 10 cabin passengers, 60 emigrants and 800 tons of freight, one roams through the stark corridors of the container ship *Atlantic Crown*. A ship of the roll on/roll off, lift on/lift off type. The main characteristic is the horizontal method of loading. The *Atlantic Crown* has six spacious decks of five wide cells to carry containers under deck. The ro/ro freight can be put on board quickly via a ramp at the back with a width of no less than $7\frac{1}{2}$ meters and a length of 15 meters. This ramp can carry loads of 60 tons and over. The ship hurries across the Atlantic with 1000 cars and 750 20-foot containers on board. The ship hurries at a speed of over 20 knots.

The Lash-ship goes again one step further. Lash-ships such as the m.v. *Bilderdijk* and the m.v. *München* were built to an original design by the fathers of this new transport system, Friede and Goldman Inc. of New Orleans. The system consists of placing barges on board a sea going vessel. A Lash-ship such as the *München* can carry 83 barges with a capacity of 375 tons each.
The barges have made us less dependent on the shore-crane. This has brought ''door-to-door'' traffic within reach. *Docklift 1* is yet one further step on the road. This first ''multi-purpose'' ship combines all new ideas on freight-carrying and sea-towage. Dredging companies and offshore drilling companies are now able to transport in a simple way non-seaworthy heavy dredging materials and prefabricated components for drilling platforms by sea with ships of the *Docklift* type. For a long time goods landed by container ships in the United States have been taken to the inland airport nearest to the consignee. There is not yet a container aircraft. But its arrival is only a question of time.

World ports too are quickly changing character. Anno 1972 Rotterdam is no longer exclusively the transit port for Western Germany, but in fact the natural point of departure for the Trans-Siberian Railway. With the large scale introduction of containers and of lash-barges, Rotterdam is beginning to lose its traditional functions. The emphasis is shifting towards accumulation and distribution rather than loading and unloading. It is now a question of cargoes from all over Europe. Lorries from Turkey and Iran are no longer an unusual sight in North European container ports.

And with the expansion of the European Economic Community, economists expect an unprecedented increase in inter-EEC traffic by road, rail, ship, and air.

One hundred years after the bridge across the Atlantic was built, a shipping company such as the Holland America Line is a diversified transport company. But the heart of the line, forever, is the ship on which people sail and smell the sea water and watch the water rise and fall and churn and dip and rush past. And always, this motion and reflections of light make it the single most wonderous view in the world. See a mountain for five minutes and you have seen it forever. Watch the ocean for a week and you only have started to be caught in its rhythm and beauty.

And the Holland America Line sends people onto the oceans aboard its brand new motor vessel *Prinsendam*, 9,150 tons gross register, a speed of 21 knots, cruise capacity for 375 passengers. Fly to Singapore by air. Board the *Prinsendam* for two weeks of cruising past

*1970

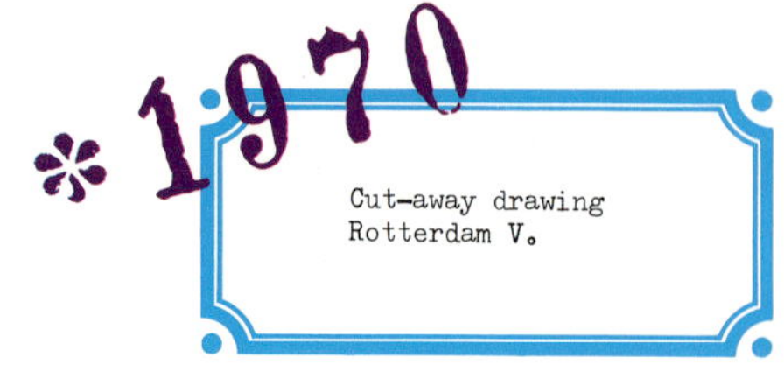

Cut-away drawing
Rotterdam V.

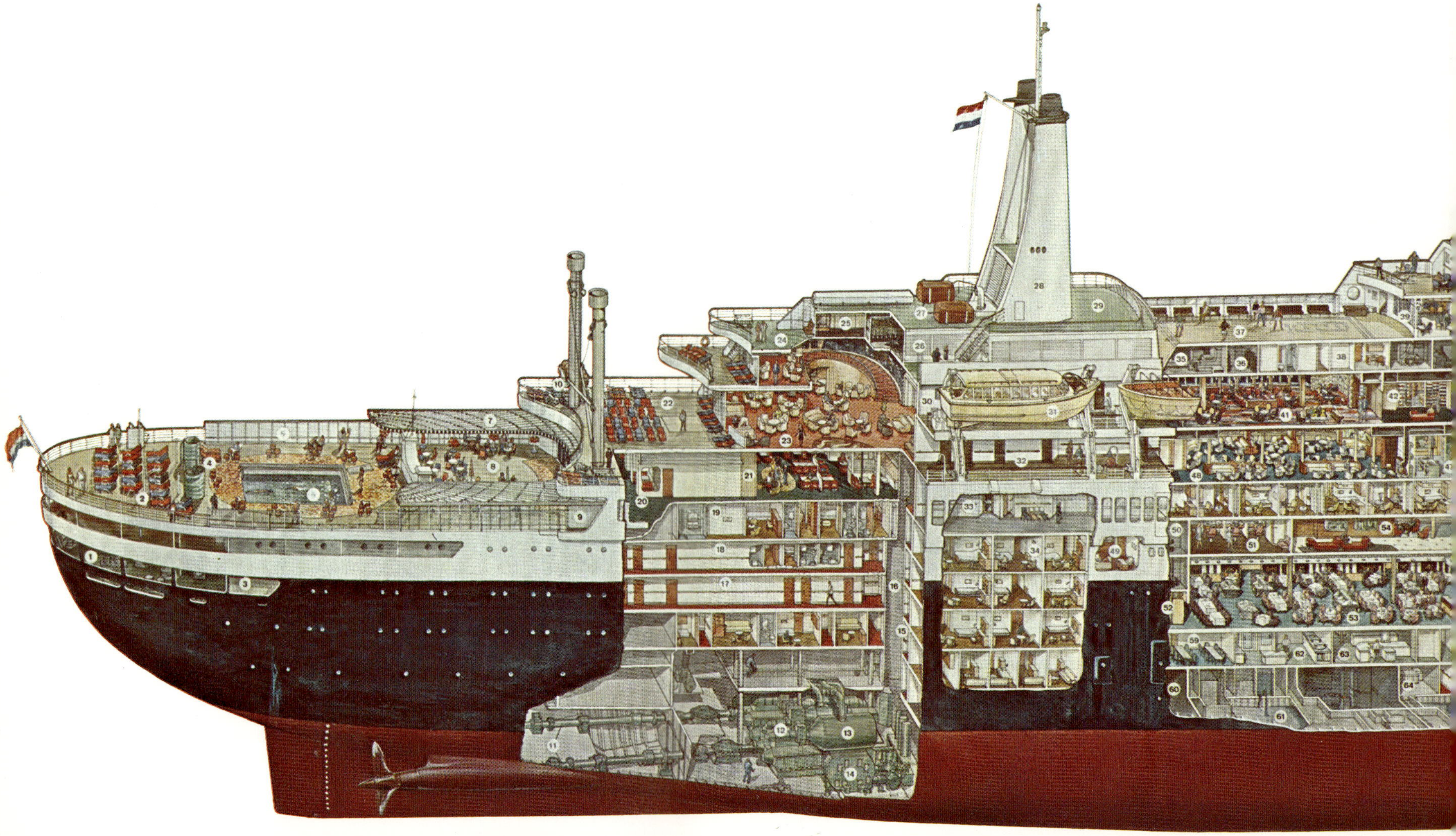

the islands of the Indonesian archipelago.

The 23,400 ton ships the *Brasilia* and the *Argentina,* acquired from Moore-MacCormack Lines, rebuilt and renamed the *Volendam* and the *Veendam,* cover the coasts of Northern and Southern Europe. And the undiscovered and the strikingly beautiful coast of East Africa.

The *Statendam,* the flagship *Rotterdam* and the Grand Old Lady of the Seas, the *Nieuw Amsterdam,* sail through the blue-green waters of the Caribbean and the vigorous, spray-covered American coast.

On cruises for peace ar d quiet, on cruises for entertainment, on cruises soon only for young people, or centering around the works of great composers and other artists for music and theatre lovers. How ever more refined and tailored to specific leisure time requirements are sea cruises becoming.

Cruising is not the boring life of the idle rich, as it once was painted. Rather, it is the place for the sea-minded. It is the place for people who see mystery in the ocean, mystery in its strength and restlessness. And cruising is the place for those who truly care to see how others live.

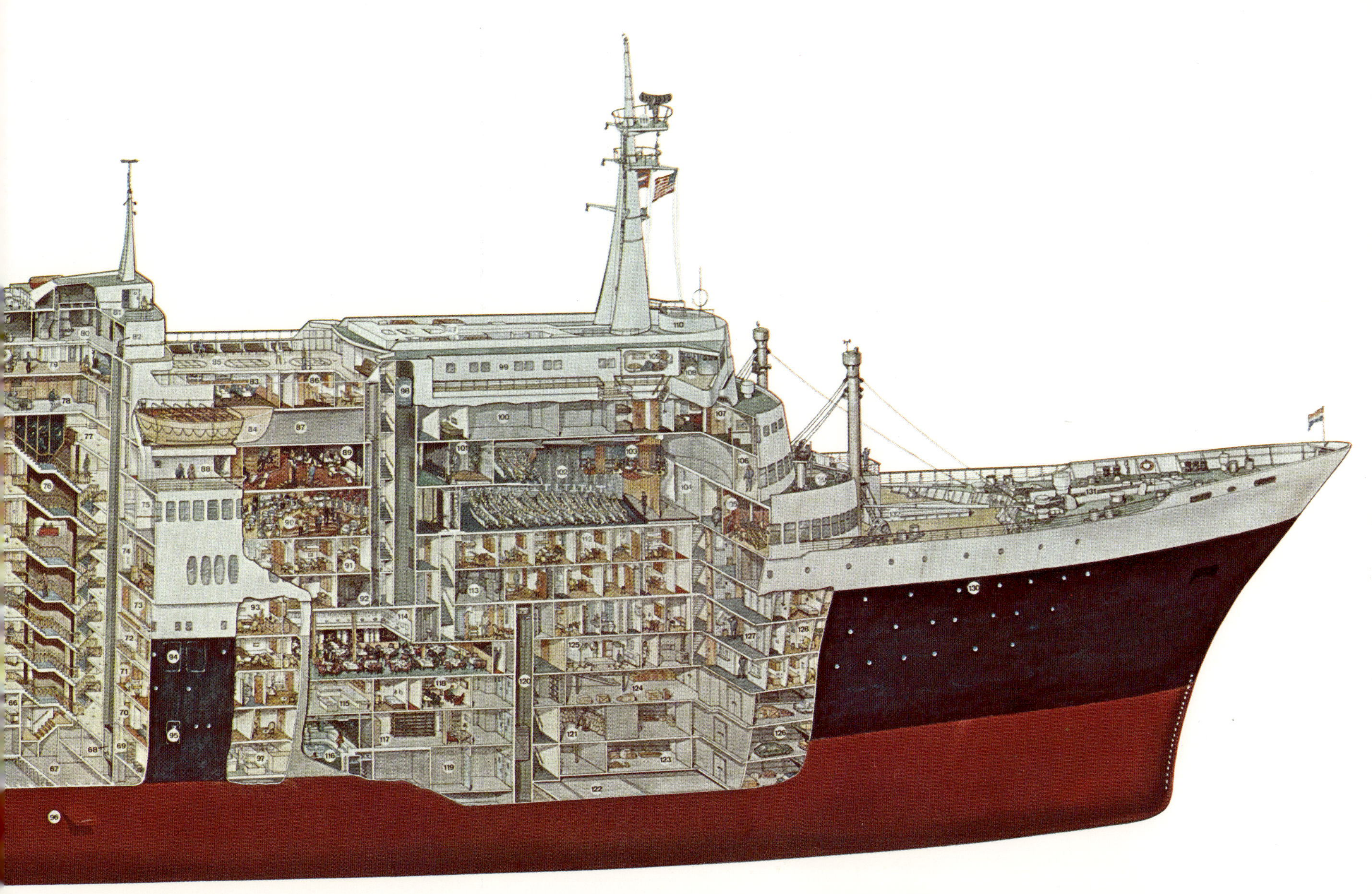

For most of the thrill of going to a place is the mere act of arriving. And not arriving all at once, in a rush through clouds and on to a runway. But arriving inch by inch. With the first darkness of the destination appearing over the horizon.

Then the island growing. Or perhaps a city growing. From the first blurred look at the parachute jump towering over Coney Island, to the top of the Verrazano spanning the harbor.
And then the island of New Amsterdam rises in front of your eyes.

The thrill is so much greater by ship. Sailing on a running tide, with the sound of water and the sight of water. For the sea is life and man can invent and conquer but he never can duplicate.

To travel. To explore the world. More and more people will be pleasure traveling by sea in the years ahead. And then returning home to tell about their double vacations : the one of incomparable atmosphere on a large and social floating ship hotel ; the one of interesting adventures away from the ship. Like meeting a fisherman with a casting net on a tropical beach, and from watching his simplicity, his patience

and his movements so completely attuned to
nature, learning more about his country and its
way of life than from running around in town
from building to monument to museum. More
and more people will cruise in the years ahead,
and more and more will they tell others that a
cruise by ship is something they will dream
about again and again as long as they live.

Even if they live to be one hundred . . .

Prinsendam (model).
Inset: Brasil and Argentina,
now Volendam and Veendam.

✻1972

✳1873-1973

One hundred years of HAL ships.

Rotterdam I
1,684 gross tons
1873–1883

Maas (Maasdam I)
1,705 gross tons
1873–1884

W. A. Scholten
2,529 gross tons
1874–1887

P. Caland
2,584 gross tons
1874–1897

Schiedam
2,236 gross tons
1877–1897

Amsterdam I
2,949 gross tons
1879–1884

Edam I
2,957 gross tons
1881–1882

Zaandam I
3,063 gross tons
1882–1897

Leerdam I
2,796 gross tons
1882–1889

Edam II
3,130 gross tons
1883–1895

Rotterdam II (Edam III)
3,329 gross tons
1886–1899

Amsterdam II
3,607 gross tons
1887–1905

Veendam I
3,707 gross tons
1888–1898

Obdam
3,699 gross tons
1889–1898

Werkendam
3,638 gross tons
1889–1900

Maasdam II
3,984 gross tons
1889–1902

Spaarndam I
4,539 gross tons
1890–1901

Didam
2,751 gross tons
1891–1895

Dubbeldam
2,700 gross tons
1891–1895

Rotterdam III
8,186 gross tons
1897–1906

Statendam I
10,491 gross tons
1898–1910

Potsdam
12,522 gross tons
1900–1915

Soestdijk I
6,445 gross tons
1901–1923

Ryndam I
12,527 gross tons
1901–1929

Amsteldyk I
6,435 gross stons
1901–1924

Sloterdyk I
6,480 gross tons
1902–1924

Noordam I
12,528 gross tons
1902–1928

Nieuw Amsterdam I
17,149 gross tons
1906–1932

Rotterdam IV
24,149 gross tons
1908–1940

Andyk I
6,292 gross tons
1909–1930

Maartensdyk
6,483 gross tons
1909–1923

Gorredyk I
6,463 gross tons
1909–1923

Zyldyk
4,190 gross tons
1909–1928

Sommelsdyk I
6,316 gross tons
1909–1910

Zaandyk I
4,189 gross tons
1909–1917

Sommelsdyk II
6,291 gross tons
1912–1930

Zuiderdyk
5,211 gross tons
1912–1922

Noorderdyk I
7,167 gross tons
1913–1917

Oosterdyk
8,251 gross tons
1913–1918

Westerdyk
8,261 gross tons
1913–1933

Veendyk
6,874 gross tons
1914–1933

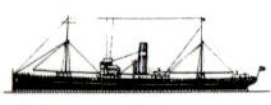
Waaldyk
4,749 gross tons
1914–1929

Maasdyk
6,065 gross tons
1915–1922

Eemdyk I
6,180 gross tons
1915

Poeldyk I
4,226 gross tons
1915–1928

Blommersdyk I
4,835 gross tons
1916

Beukelsdyk
6,801 gross tons
1916–1923

Yseldyk
7,157 gross tons
1916–1926

Statendam II (Justicia)
32,234 gross tons
— — —

Schiedyk I
7,046 gross tons
1917–1926

Zaandyk II
4,512 gross tons
1918–1923

Stadsdyk
6,744 gross tons
1920–1932

Noorderdyk II
8,384 gross tons
1918–1932

Moerdyk I
7,310 gross tons
1915–1933

Kinderdyk I
7,651 gross tons
1915–1933

Eemdyk II
7,655 gross tons
1915–1933

Vechtdyk
6,869 gross tons
1920–1933

Warszawa
4,321 gross tons
1920–1926

Burgerdyk
6,853 gross tons
1921–1940

Maasdam III
8,812 gross tons
1921–1941

Edam IV
8,871 gross tons
1921–1954

Leerdam II
8,854 gross tons
1921–1953

Blydendyk I
6,854 gross tons
1921–1930

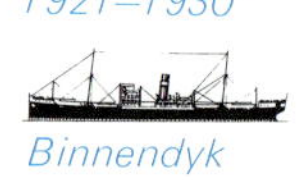
Binnendyk
6,873 gross tons
1921–1939

Dinteldyk I
9,399 gross tons
1922–1946

Breedyk
6,861 gross tons
1922–1942

Spaarndam II
8,857 gross tons
1922–1939

Volendam I
15,434 gross tons
1922–1952

Gaasterdyk I
8,373 gross tons
1922–1931

Bilderdyk I
6,856 gross tons
1922–1940

Beemsterdyk
6,869 gross tons
1922–1941

Grootendyk
8,365 gross tons
1923–1931

Drechtdyk
9,338 gross tons
1923–1947

Veendam II
15,450 gross tons
1923–1953

Boschdyk
6,872 gross tons
1922–1940

Blommersdyk II
6,855 gross tons
1922–1957

Statendam III
29,511 gross tons
1929–1940

Delftdyk (Dongedyk)
10,220 gross tons
1929–1966

Damsterdyk (Dalerdyk)
10,155 gross tons
1930–1963

Nieuw Amsterdam II
36,287 gross tons
1938–

Noordam II
10,726 gross tons
1938–1963

Zaandam II
10,909 gross tons
1938–1942

Westernland
16,479 gross tons
1939–1943

Pennland
16,381 gross tons
1939–1941

Sommelsdyk III
9,227 gross tons
1939–1965

Sloterdyk II
9,230 gross tons
1940–1966

Westerdam
12,149 gross tons
1946–1964

Zuiderdam
12,150 gross tons
— — —

Andyk II
8,380 gross tons
1946–1969

Eemdyk III
9,894 gross tons
1946–1960

Amsteldyk II
7,648 gross tons
1946–1967

Duivendyk
8,338 gross tons
1946–1959

Arkeldyk
7,664 gross tons
1946–1966

Aalsdyk
7,645 gross tons
1946–1960

Averdyk
7,646 gross tons
1947–1967

Abbedyk
7,640 gross tons
1947–1961

Axeldyk
7,639 gross tons
1947–1962

Aardyk
7,643 gross tons
1947–1962

Blydendyk II
7,231 gross tons
1947–1957

Arnedyk
7,638 gross tons
1947–1962

Alblasserdyk
8,292 gross tons
1948–1966

Arendsdyk
7,639 gross tons
1948–1961

Soestdyk II
9,592 gross tons
1948–1967

Akkrumdyk
7,639 gross tons
1948–1962

Almdyk
8,286 gross tons
1948–1965

Schiedyk
9,592 gross tons
1949–1968

Aagtedyk
7,646 gross tons
1950–1963

Diemerdyk
11,195 gross tons
1950–1968

Ryndam II
15,015 gross tons
1951–1972

Maasdam IV
15,024 gross tons
1952–1968

Appingedyk
7,624 gross tons
1952–1962

Kinderdyk II
5,634 gross tons
1956–1970

Statendam IV
24,294 gross tons
1957–

Dinteldyk II
11,366 gross tons
1957–1970

Kloosterdyk
5,635 gross tons
1957–1970

Kerkedyk
5,324 gross tons
1958–1970

Kamperdyk (Volta Peace)
5,290 gross tons
1959–

Rotterdam V
38,645 gross tons
1959–

Korendyk (Volta Wisdom)
5,290 gross tons
1960–

Gaasterdyk II
7,222 gross tons
1960–

Katsedyk
5,376 gross tons
1961–

Grebbedyk
7,259 gross tons
1962–

Grotedyk
7,251 gross tons
1962–

Gorredyk II
7,298 gross tons
1962–

Poeldyk II
3,551 gross tons
1964–

Prinses Margriet
9,336 gross tons
1964–1970

Moerdyk II
11,127 gross tons
1965–

Atlantic Star
11,839 gross tons
1967–

Atlantic Crown
15,469 gross tons
1969–

Bilderdyk II
36,974 gross tons
1972–

Docklift 1
2,594 gross tons
1972–

Volendam II
23,400 gross tons
1973–

Veendam III
23,400 gross tons
1973–

Prinsendam
9,150 gross tons
1973–

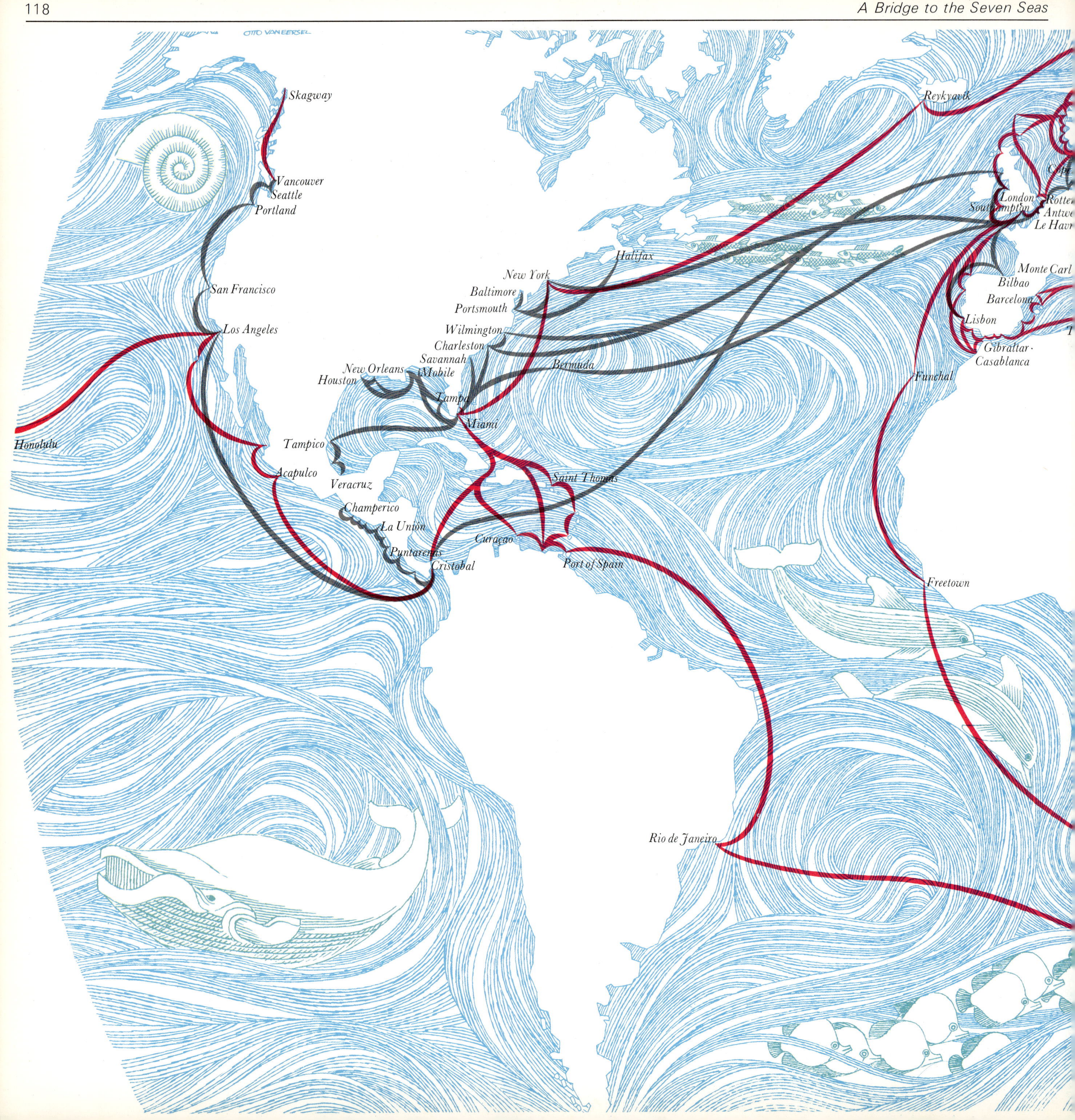
OTTO VAN EERSEL
Skagway
Vancouver
Seattle
Portland
San Francisco
Los Angeles
Honolulu
Tampico
Acapulco
Veracruz
Champerico
La Unión
Puntarenas
Cristobal
Houston
New Orleans
Mobile
Savannah
Charleston
Wilmington
Portsmouth
Baltimore
New York
Halifax
Tampa
Miami
Bermuda
Saint Thomas
Curaçao
Port of Spain
Rio de Janeiro
Freetown
Reykjavik
London
Southampton
Rotter
Antwe
Le Havr
Monte Carl
Bilbao
Barcelona
Lisbon
Gibraltar
Casablanca
Funchal

Freight
Cruises
*1973

North Cape
Helsinki
Leningrad
holm
rg
me
Naples
Istanbul
Piraeus
Haifa.
ta
Nagasaki
Kōbe
Yokohama
Hong Kong
Bombay
Madras
Bangkok
Cochin
Colombo
Belawan
Penang
Mombasa
Singapore
Djakarta
Bali
Beira
Walvis Bay
Durban
Cape Town

Drawings pages 116/117:
D. G. D. Haws
Map pages 118/119:
Otto van Eersel
Design, and editing of illustrations
Will van Sambeek Design Associates
Production:
Meijer Pers bv, Amsterdam, the Netherlands
Lithographs:
NV Koningsveld & Zoon, Leiden, the Netherlands
Printed by:
Drukkerij Meijer Wormerveer bv, Wormerveer, the Netherlands
Binding:
Binderij Callenbach nv, Nijkerk, the Netherlands